The
Captain's Daughters
of Martha's Vineyard

The daughters

Nina Eldridge	1878 — 1960
Mary Eldridge Macy	1880 — 1978
Ruth Eldridge White	1883 — 1967
Gratia Eldridge Harrington	1885 —

The Captain's Daughters

of Martha's Vineyard

As recalled by the Eldridge sisters
Nina • Mary • Ruth • Gratia

Edited by

Eliot Eldridge Macy

The Chatham Press

Distributed by The Devin-Adair Company
Old Greenwich, Connecticut

Library of Congress Catalogue Card No. 78-62650
ISBN: 0-85699-141-4 (hard cover)
       0-85699-142-2 (paperback)

Canadian agent: Beaverbooks Ltd., Pickering, Ont.

Printed in the United States of America

CONTENTS

Acknowledgments		vii
Foreword		ix
I	Early Childhood, The Chandlery	1
II	School	15
III	After School	27
IV	Grandfather, Father, and Sardines	35
V	Playmates	49
VI	Rules and Duties	61
VII	Jaunts	71
VIII	Christian Charity	75
IX	The Barracks	81
X	Boarders	85
XI	Limes and Loafing Places	87
XII	The Church	95
XIII	Christmas	103
XIV	Menemsha	109
XV	Visiting Dignitaries	113
XVI	Rich and Poor	121
XVII	Politics	127
XVIII	Storm	131
XIX	Love Story	137
Afterword		145
Appendix I	ELDRIDGE TIDES & PILOT BOOK	153
Appendix II	GREATEST STORM OF THE XIX CENTURY	157
	Map of Vineyard Haven	92
	Island Map	111
	Photographs between pages 116 and 117	

Acknowledgments

It was Sydna White, firstborn of our generation, who succeeded finally in getting her mother Ruth to sit down and put on paper the stories about her girlhood that have been woven into this book. I am indebted to Sydna, and to Isabel (White) West and Gordon and Robert White, not only for their permission to use these stories, but also for their thoughtful reading of the manuscript at various stages of its development and for coming up with timely corrections and numerous fruitful suggestions.

For pictures I want to thank Constance Fuller Sanborn and Stanton Lair, who generously made available prints they have collected for a forthcoming book of their own; Mrs. Muriel C. Crossman, Librarian of the Dukes County Historical Society, who searched the archives long and diligently for scenes of the Great Storm of '98; Mrs. Kenneth Stoddard, President of the Historical Society; Thomas E. Norton, Director of the Historical Museum; and Hollis Engley.

I thank Elinor McCabe for drawing the maps, which show the principal places mentioned by the daughters.

I thank the *Vineyard Gazette* for making available from its files the newspaper account of the Great Storm.

I especially thank Sara Crafts and Kyra West for typing and preparing the manuscript and going along with everlasting changes with unfailing patience and good humor.

Above all, I wish to acknowledge my indebtedness to my good friends and partners in creation, Lewis McCabe and Lucy Reynolds. Lewis foresaw the possibilities of a book and gave it its first form. Lucy's skill as a writer was an invaluable resource. To a large extent this book should be viewed as our combined effort.

Foreword

In December, 1850, George Eldridge of Chatham, Mas-sachusetts, was thrown violently from the mainmast to the deck as his coasting schooner tossed in gale winds and lashing waves. The fall left him with a permanent stoop and took away his livelihood.

In April the following year the ebb current of another great storm formed dangerous new shoals off Chatham that were named Chatham New Harbor Bars. A nun buoy was set to show their general location, but at night the mariner had neither mark nor bearing to guide him. And since the new shoals lay directly in the track of schooners carrying heavy freight between Boston and New York and ports beyond, they were, George Eldridge felt, "the most dangerous spot on the coast of the United States." He decided to do something about it.

Although he was still convalescing from his accident, he rowed out in a dory and began taking soundings. Day after day, patiently, doggedly, he persisted. In time he was able to put together a rough, large-scale chart of the Chatham New Harbor Bars. When he showed it to fellow mariners they were immediately eager to know when it was to be published so they could have a copy. Two features about it they especially liked. It was large scale, so easy to read under emergency conditions in ill-lit cabins. And it was, contrary to convention, made with South at the top and North at the bottom. This made it easier for the southbound skipper who had to probe for the deepwater needle in shoal-strewn Nantucket Sound and tack back and forth against prevailing southerly winds. The skipper exiting from the Sound had a relatively easy downwind run.

The chart was published, and with it began a family business that continues and flourishes today in the form of the annually published *Eldridge Tide and Pilot Book*.

"Chart George" had a son, George Washington Eldridge. In his twenties the latter made his living by sailing a small catboat around to the various ports near Chatham to sell his father's charts. Most of his time was spent at Vineyard Haven on Martha's Vineyard, for Vineyard Haven Harbor was the principal stopping place between Boston and New York for coasting vessels. As he went from schooner to schooner, he was frequently asked: "When does the current change in the Sound?" From this he conceived the idea of a tidebook specifically for Vineyard Sound and other strategic areas. His father liked the idea, and in 1875 the first *Eldridge Tide and Pilot Book* was published. Its cover was green, it had 64 pages, and it sold for fifty cents.

That same year George W. and Sydna Saurbaugh of Bridgeville, Ohio, were married. They came to Vineyard Haven, bought a house down-the-Neck, and had four daughters — Nina, Mary, Ruth, and Gratia.

George W. loved the Vineyard, was good at getting to know people, and soon became a well-known Island figure. Everyone called him Captain Eldridge. But he was a restless man, his head teemed with ideas, and he found staying in one place oppressive. After fifteen years as a ship's chandler, a disastrous stint as president of a harness factory (during which he lost most of his money), he decided to start his own chart publishing business.

With the Captain away much of the time from 1890 on, the Eldridge girls grew up very much in a woman's world. This was more so because Sydna Eldridge, their mother, was no ordinary woman. She was an activist, and she saw much to be set right in the world. It was not uncommon for the girls to come down in the morning and find her deeply engrossed in a letter to her congressman or working over a paper she would read at some forthcoming meeting. When they asked her if breakfast was ready, she would say, "Well, the eggs are ready to be cooked." Sydna grew up on a small Ohio farm. She taught school before marrying, and somewhere along the line firmly acquired the notion that she, a woman, was a person as much as any man. Not that she was a George Sand. Her style was gentler. She was also practical — more concerned with such things as upgrading the school and stamping out alcoholism than she was with confronting male prejudice. She knew she was equal, and that was enough. Her daughters reflected the same assurance.

Her third daughter, Ruth's, flair for storytelling came from her father. The Captain was said to be a master storyteller. He was in Gloucester on business once at the time Rudyard Kipling was there gathering material for *Captain's Courageous*. Kipling and he were at the same hotel and became acquainted. After dinner in the evening George would join Kipling in his room and regale him with sea stories. Some of us like to say that George practically wrote *Captain's Courageous* — a ridiculous exaggeration of course — yet he must have had an influence. When the book came out, certain people were heard to exclaim: "Why, this isn't Gloucester! This is Cape Cod!"

I suppose every family has a story somewhere, but few of them get written down and fewer still end up in print. For saving these memories from oblivion, major credit must go to Lewis McCabe. On a certain summer evening he discovered Gratia, youngest of the sisters, at a dinner party. She was then eighty-eight. What caught his attention was not her age but her vitality. She was easily the liveliest person at the party and seemed to know a great deal about the Vineyard as she recalled the early days in great detail. When Lewis and I met later that summer, he remarked to me that someone really ought to get Gratia's recollections down on tape. I thought to myself how nice that somebody could find dear Auntie so interesting and said, oh, yes, by all means — the way one does. Some weeks later I received in the mail from Lewis six hour-long tapes of Gratia's recollections. I listened to them, dutifully at first, and then with increasing interest and respect.

Transcribing them became a kind of hobby, something mainly for the family. Then we found that Ruth had left some reminiscences, and Nina had written a long article about the old chandlery. Mary, my mother, four years Gratia's senior, had some recollections of her own to add. Ultimately, Lewis McCabe and Lucy Reynolds, with their perceptive criticisms and unflagging enthusiasm and encouragement, came at just the right time, sat down and worked the various pieces together.

So then, this is the way it was on the Vineyard in the 1880's and '90's — at least as seen by Nina, a person of many moods, Mary, who wanted more than anything to be good, Ruth, who had imagination and beauty, and Gratia, who fortunately remembers everything.

ELIOT ELDRIDGE MACY

Vineyard Haven, Mass.

I
Early Childhood, The Chandlery

RUTH: If in the 1880's you started to walk the road to West Chop from the village of Vineyard Haven, called in those days "the head," because it was the head of the harbor, you would be inclined to stop halfway for a rest. You stopped partly because you were tired from walking through heavy sand and partly because you had come to an ancient graveyard, which seemed a natural place for one to stop, rest, and consider. Here slept the departed neighbors of "down-the-Neck": CAPT. CLIFFORD DUNHAM, DIED AT HAVANA, CUBA 1851 . . . LEONARD CLEVELAND, LOST NEAR FAYAL 1853 . . . THOMAS LUCE, DIED AT CALLAO, PERU 1849 . . . NORA, AGE 21 DIED IN CHILDBIRTH. Close beside her lay her baby in its everlasting cradle. In the center of the graveyard stood an impressive monument with an urn on top, but only BELOVED HUSBAND . . . BELOVED WIFE told the story.

To the rear of the place was a grove of pine and oak trees. The cleared land was planted with fruit trees, mostly russet and greening apples, and in summer a vegetable garden spread out on the eastern slope.

GRATIA: February 25, 1885, was a cold, snowy day, and the harbor was frozen over. The doctor who was to deliver Mother had to come from the head of the harbor to the Neck, where we then lived. It wasn't practical for him to come by horse and buggy, so he skated down the harbor on his skates. Poor doctor, he hardly dared tell Mother I was another girl. She already had three girls, and she had wanted all boys. When she saw me, she greeted me by exclaiming, "Oh, you poor homely little thing!" Mother, I must confess, saw my name in a book and liked it. It's particularly ironic, because she was so sorry I was a girl and *gratia* is Latin for "thanks."

Now in those days there was, of course, the village at the head of the harbor. Then, proceeding toward West Chop, there was the Neck, and then West Chop. People living down-the-Neck always spoke of "going to the head" when they were going to the village. In those days there was no breakwater to mar our beautiful harbor. And it was not uncommon to see two hundred sail at anchor, for Vineyard Haven was the finest harbor of refuge between New York and Boston. Many sail anchored here waiting for fair wind and a fair tide before going across the treacherous Nantucket Shoals and around the Cape to Boston.

There is a sailor's hell,
There is a sailor's heaven;
One is Nantucket Shoals,
The other is Vineyard Haven.

I've heard that on occasion as many as two thousand sail passed along Vineyard Sound between Woods Hole and

Vineyard Haven in one day. At that time they had a man on the lookout with a spyglass who more or less kept tabs on the vessels that passed back and forth. That's probably why they had a pretty accurate idea of the number.

Vineyard Haven used to be called Holmes Hole. In old records you'll find the spelling "Homes" Hole. "Homes" is an Indian word meaning "old man," "hole" means deep water, safe anchorage. Later they made it Holmes Hole after the Holmes family. But people didn't like the name. And who can blame them? It's not a euphonious sound. I've always liked "Whitsun Bay." They say Gosnold named it that because it was Whitsunday the day he sailed into the harbor. Anyway, the townspeople decided they wanted a new name, and a contest was held. A woman who lived in a big house by Owen Park, a Mrs. Crocker, came up with Vineyard Haven, and that's what it has been called ever since.

The vessels in the harbor came from all over. We not only had coasting vessels — ships that sailed up and down the coast; we also had deepsea voyagers, including ships of foreign registry. We had a customs office in the town then. Vineyard Haven was sea oriented. There was no division between Tisbury and West Tisbury. There were fishermen and whaling people. There was still some whaling in the eighties and nineties.

At the time Father owned a ship's chandlery at the end of Grove Street and on the water, about a two-minute walk down from our house. It was an old, old building and had been a ship's chandlery for a long time.

MARY: Nina was a precocious, independent child. One day, when she was only two and a half, Mother called for her to come to lunch and she didn't answer. She was not in any of the usual places she liked to play. Once when she was a year and a half she had walked down to the chandlery all by herself. Father had reprimanded her most severely, and it seemed unlikely she would do it again. Still, Mother thought, she might have forgotten.

Mother came and got me (all of seven months at the time), picked me up in her arms, and hurried down to the chandlery. But Nina was not there. Although Mother was usually a very calm person, now she became alarmed. Father told her to go back to the house and look after me, and said he would go in search. And search he did.

He went to all the neighbors, but none of them had seen Nina. He decided she must have gone into the woods. He went out among the ships in the harbor and asked sailors to help in the search, and they gladly responded. He went into the village. The church bells were rung, and children were let out of school to join the search.

Supper passed and night came on, and still there was no sign of Nina. A number of people stayed with Father and continued the search by lantern light through the night.

In the early morning Father decided they had not gone far enough and that they should form a human rake of themselves and walk straight west into the woods. Finally, about six o'clock, a sailor found Nina sound asleep under a huckleberry bush with a bunch of flowers clutched in her hand. She loved the forest flowers and had become so absorbed in picking she hadn't realized how far from home she had strayed — nearly a mile. She had a few scratches here and there, but otherwise was unharmed. The sailor lifted her up on his shoulders, and there was great rejoicing.

NINA: There's a house on the site where the old chandlery used to be. They call it the Anchorage. Until a few years ago you could see stumps of old spiles that carried the wharf out into the harbor. Now even these are gone. But I can still see everything as it was. For the first ten years of my life the store was the place where all my really living hours were spent. It was my playground, my school, and always my point of departure for imagined journeys out upon the dark and mysterious sea.

Father bought the store from the Holmes family in 1879 when I was a year old, and it was ancient even then. The floor sagged, and none of its walls were plumb. No one knew how old it was or who built it. Perhaps you wonder why it was built so far from the head of the harbor and the village. The answer is, down-the-Neck, as they called it, was where all the big ships dropped anchor. In those days our harbor was the most important port-of-call on the New England coast. As many as 35,000 vessels a year might pass through Vineyard Sound — two-, three- and four-masted schooners carrying lumber, coal, lime, cement, and other such bulky freight from as far north as Halifax to Norfolk in the south and beyond. Some of the schooners were ocean-going and had foreign registry. Ships arrived on every tide by the score, and when the wind was right you could hear the running clank of their anchor chains in the hawseholes and the rattle of masthoops as their sails were lowered. Some stopped for water and provisions, some for repairs and gear, others just for papers and mail or to wait for fair tide and winds.

The chandlery itself — there were several small sheds besides — was forty feet north and south, somewhat less east and west, and faced the harbor with a two-story front.

It was not a large building, but it contained just about everything a sailing ship or her crew might need — rope of all sizes, both manila and tarred hemp, anchors, capstans, foghorns, bilge pumps, tackle blocks, lanterns, flares, oilskins, boots, fine nautical instruments (kept in glass cases), and, of course, an up-to-date supply of Eldridge and government charts and the *Tidebook*. There was a food section too. The range of choice was considerably less than in a modern supermarket, but it was sufficiently broad to serve the needs of the usual ship's galley. Nearly everything was sold in bulk from barrels and bins. About the only things sold in cans were salmon and condensed milk.

But perhaps the two most important things found at the old chandlery were the paper and mail. There was a big sign on the harbor side, which covered the second story from one end to the other. You could read the words a mile away: NEW YORK HERALD SOLD HERE. The paper was important to seamen because of the shipping news. As for the mail, although the chandlery was not a post office, it was the one place the sailor was sure to go. For this reason all shipping mail was sent in the chandlery's care, and each day a batch of it came down from the village post office. To the left as one entered harborside was a wire rack stuck full of sailors' letters. They bore all sorts of postmarks, foreign and domestic.

It was a man's store, no place for a woman, and none was ever seen there. The sailors who came in lived a life with few comforts aboardship, and they were a rough lot. They always wore a sheath knife at the hip, and you could see the tip of of the sheath extending below the hem of their pea jackets. They came in for their mail and for tobacco and candy. They were not supposed to roam the neighborhood, but naturally they did. They foraged for blueberries and apples and especially for cats. A ship without a cat was considered bad luck. Thus, when sailors were ashore, we all kept close watch of our cats. Nevertheless, some disappeared anyway, causing tears and heartaches. But Father taught us to think kindly of the poor sailors. He had been to sea as a young man and knew how hard the life could be, especially in the middle of a howling nor'easter, so we at our house quite forgave them for stealing our kittens.

The ships' captains were another breed of men altogether. They were dignified, well spoken, even learned, and some became good friends with Father. They would spend long hours together talking about their experiences at sea. Occasionally the captains brought gifts for the family, beautiful, polished shells and exotic fruits from faraway places. For Father the gift was likely to be a tall jug of rum or gin, which he always graciously accepted though he was a teetotaler. He was not opposed to drinking. He had simply never developed a taste for it.

Every captain who came in had the same three questions put to him: "Where're you from? Where're you bound? Who's your consignee?" Halifax, Yarmouth, Eastport, Belfast, Rockland, Machias, Bath, Portland, Boston, New London, Bridgeport, New York, Perth Amboy, Philadelphia, Wilmington, Baltimore, Norfolk — I could soon rattle off the coastal ports backwards and forwards, though perhaps not in the proper geographical order. The word consignee puzzled me somewhat. From the context and its sound I formed the picture of an odd-looking man at the end of the journey with a large knee.

The old store was a wonderful place to play, especially in bad weather. The coziest corner was under the north eaves, close to the chimney, where it was warm and where there were stored a few old relics from various shipwrecks. There were several seachests, an old trunk, and a rusty sewing machine.

In fine weather, of course, I preferred the out-of-doors. A plank walk led from the store to the wharf. At its end was a derrick for hoisting heavy gear. The wharf itself was well loaded with big anchors and heavy chains. There were men who made a business of anchor-dragging, recovering lost chains and anchors from the harbor bottom. They would chip off the rust, paint them, and sell them again.

There were no easy landing stages from the wharf to the water. You had to get from the one to the other by wooden ladders, the length of the climb depending upon the height of the tide. On occasion my sisters and I were permitted to scramble down the ladder that led to Father's Osterville-built Crosby catboat and play dolls in the cockpit. Or Father might take us with him as he sailed out to make an official inspection of a ship's damage for the underwriter. At a very young age we learned how to hold the tiller, steer by a mark, know the difference between sheet and toppinglift, make fast throat, and peak halyards without jamming the rope in the cleats. Sometimes, when the boat was tied at the wharf, we just leaned over the sides and watched the wave shadows dancing over the golden sand on the bottom, the brown rocks, the wavering seaweed and darting minnows.

One winter the harbor was frozen over, and a sizable fleet was icebound for weeks. I remember walking over the ice holding onto Father's hand as he visited various captains. I marveled at the snug cabins and the way the ship rocked in the tide underneath the ice. It was then I learned the new word "ratlines," which the sailors obligingly climbed for my amusement.

Another winter experience was all my own. One morning I was told suddenly I must not under any circumstances go near the chandlery. This was most unusual. In fact, it had never happened before. Father said he liked having me in the store with him. He said the sailors behaved better when I was there. I couldn't understand it. But I knew better than to question Father. He was terrifying when he was angry, and sometimes it took very little to provoke him.

Later in the day I overheard Mother and a neighbor quietly talking, and caught enough to deduce that something was being brought to the chandlery from some sunken ship. This excited me greatly, for I at once imagined that this something must be a treasure. I wanted passionately to see the treasure. I went outside to a place behind our house where the ground was high and from where in winter, with no leaves on the trees, you had a view of the chandlery. I could see nothing, I was too far away. I could see the chandlery, all right, but not *into* it. I was on the point of turning away when my eye fell upon a mysterious mound at the end of the wharf covered over with what looked like an old sail. It was the treasure, I thought, I just knew it. And perhaps it was ours! Wasn't it ours if it was on our wharf? Perhaps Father was keeping it for a surprise. He loved springing surprises on us. The possibilities were dizzying.

I wanted to whirl about and turn somersaults and run down the hill and dance and sing and shout. I contained myself, however, for I thought that if Mother or Father found out I knew the secret, the treasure might somehow vanish into thin air. I vowed to be especially good all the rest of the day. I took extra pains not to spill any food at supper. I waited patiently for Father to come home from the chandlery. Surely then he would announce the surprise.

But Father didn't come home, and he didn't come home, and then Mother said it was time to go to bed. "But what about the surprise?" I blurted out, unable to contain myself any longer.

"Surprise, Nina? There's no surprise. Whatever gave you the idea there was a surprise, child?"

I could only shake my head helplessly. Mother immediately saw how disappointed I was and took pity on me. She gave Mary and me each a candy — Ruth was only a baby then and Gratia was not yet born — and we went dutifully to bed.

I couldn't sleep. I couldn't stop thinking about the treasure. It wasn't the disapppointment. I got over that quickly enough. After all, it was expecting far too much, expecting the treasure to be ours. What kept me awake, what gnawed at my mind all night long, was the thought that the treasure might be taken away and I wouldn't have a chance even to see it.

In the morning, as soon as it was barely light, I got up. I put on my clothes and stole out of the house and made for the chandlery. It was bitter cold. There was snow on the ground from a recent fall, and on the path where it was packed my shoes made a creaking sound at every step. I was in a panic that someone would hear me and stop me. But no one did. I reached the chandlery safely and went out on the wharf. There was not *one* mound, there were *three* mounds! Each was about as high as I was tall, and each was covered with a canvas. The canvases were held down by short pieces of heavy wood placed at intervals around the base. Most of the wood pieces were too heavy for me or they were frozen too solidly to the wharf, but finally I found a place where I could dislodge enough pieces to get the canvas free. When I lifted the canvas, I found row upon row of frozen bodies! (Years later I learned they were from the ill-starred *City of Columbus*, which was wrecked on Devil's Bridge just off Gay Head. The bodies had been brought to our wharf for identification and claiming.)

Do you think I was frightened and horrified? If I had been a little older, perhaps I might have been. But I was too young to have any conception of death as a reality that might touch me. I was not frightened; I was fascinated by the bodies. I touched their faces. They felt like the cold marble headstones in the cemetery at the top of our lane, only colder and smoother. I thought they were beautiful.

I let the canvas fall back over the bodies and replaced the pieces of wood. Walking back up the hill to our house I thought to myself, now this belongs to me alone, no one else knows about it. Only I know about the beautiful marble people.

RUTH: When the foghorn blew and seagulls were crying overhead, I would feel unbearably lonely. Then I would remember what Mama said, and it wasn't so bad. She said the foghorn was calling all captains and sailors, telling them not to be afraid when they felt lost in the fog. Once I was boxberrying with Nina and Mary, and we got separated. I couldn't find them, they couldn't find me. I was afraid nobody would ever find me. It began to get dark, and I cried and cried. Then I heard Papa's voice calling to me! Mama said the foghorn sounds to sailors just the way Papa's voice sounded to me that time. "I'll give you a little verse to remember," Mama said:

Ho, Mr. Captain! Oh there you be!
Hark, Mr. Captain! And here I be!
Don't be afraid on the foggy sea,
You're safer than safe if you listen to me.

GRATIA: Father had a sister, Aunt Abbey, and after her husband died, she came to live with us. Father had a room added to the house for her. Her husband had been a successful Chatham doctor, especially popular with women patients, and although Aunt Abbey herself was a beautiful woman, she suffered terribly from jealousy. She was a difficult woman, very spoiled, and she had moods. After several years of having her in the house, Mother couldn't stand it anymore. Then Father got his brothers Howard and Hiram to build Aunt Abbey a house on William Street in the village and moved her there. She was thrown from her carriage and injured. She went to bed and stayed there. She became very paranoid and wouldn't eat, and eventually starved herself to death.

RUTH: When it was time for me to go to school, Father sold the old Holmes place down-the-Neck, and we moved into a house in the village, the house formerly occupied by Father's sister.

GRATIA: I was five when we moved from the Neck to the head of the harbor. Our new home was on William Street, the section that goes toward the cemetery, two city blocks up from the big turn on the left. We called that big turn just beyond Spring Street "Lambert's Corner." There used to be a hitching post there. I remember when we moved. In those days moving was done by drays. A dray was a long platform with four wheels drawn by a horse or a pair of horses. Our furniture was piled on a dray. There was a sofa, and I sat on the sofa on the dray. I thought it was a very exciting performance.

II
School

GRATIA: The village schoolhouse stood on the ground now occupied by the town tennis courts. It stood back from Centre Street about seventy-five feet on a slight rise, a two-story, gabled building with pilasters decorating the façade. It was painted a dull brown with a darker brown for the trim. A square belfry sat atop the gable and housed the school bell.

The school had three rooms, primary and intermediate rooms downstairs, grammar room upstairs. Each room had three classes. You didn't call them grades; that came later. You started in the primary room in the third class, proceeded to the second, then the first, and then you repeated the same pattern in the intermediate and grammar rooms respectively. There was no high school yet, but anyone who wanted studies beyond the third year of the grammar room was provided for. Some algebra was taught, some Latin, though in a very haphazard way.

RUTH: The primary teacher was Mrs. Dunham. The first thing she did was ask you to stand and say your name so she could write it down for the daily roll call. One by one the children gave their names. As I listened, I noticed each gave *three* names, a first, a last, and a middle — like Lizzie Norton Jones. I thought: Whatever *will* I do when my turn comes? I have just *two* names, Ruth Eldridge.

As my turn grew closer and closer, I was near to tears. Then, in the nick of time, my good angel swooped down and whispered in my ear: "You had an Aunt Abbey Rose, remember? Why can't you be Ruth Rose?"

My turn came. "My name is Ruth Rose Eldridge," I announced uncertainly.

"A little louder, please," Mrs. Dunham said. "We didn't hear your middle name."

I shouted it so all the children could hear. "My name is Ruth ROSE Eldridge!"

GRATIA: My time to start school came in September, 1891, when I was six. Nina, Mary, and Ruth had been urging me to let them teach me how to read, but I refused, maintaining stoutly that school was the place to learn, home wasn't. However, as the fateful day approached, I began to have misgivings, and when it arrived I told Mother she had to go with me. She tried to put me off by saying that Nina and Mary would take very good care of me. But I persisted. Finally I confessed I wanted her to go to explain to the teacher that I didn't know much anyway. She consented.

Mrs. Dunham, the teacher, was standing in the doorway when we arrived. I can see her now perfectly. She was a big woman with white hair, which she wore in a French twist with a fringe across the forehead. It was a favorite hairstyle then. She wore a gray skirt with white lines in it, very long, of course, and she wore a basque. A basque was a boned garment that came to a point over the skirt. Hers was trimmed with black rickrack. Mrs. Dunham and Mother were friends, and when Mother explained why she came, they both laughed. I was insulted.

I had always understood that C-A-T was the first word you learned in school. When the teacher wrote M-A-T on the board instead, I was most indignant.

I had a stormy time at school from the very beginning. One day Mrs. Dunham told me to do something and I mumbled under my breath. "What did you say?" she asked. "I won't if I don't want to," I said. "You'll lose a week's recess," she said. I mumbled again. "What did you say?" she asked. "I won't if I don't want to," I said. "Two weeks' recess," she said. I stopped right there. I was a lively child, and it was hard for me to sit still in school. To lose recesses in addition was more than I could bear.

When I came to school the third year, Mrs. Dunham told me I was not to be in the primary room any longer, but was to skip third class and go into the intermediate room. I found that very exciting.

The intermediate room was taught by a most charming lady named Hursell. She lived on William Street in the house the Pangburns now have. Her father built that house. There was tuberculosis in her family; all her family died of it. Once a large family, only a brother and a sister were left. She had a real genius for teaching, she made school a joy. She maintained good discipline, yet made us love to go to school. One interesting feature of her classes was telling proverbs. She would have us tell as many as we could in five minutes. I believe once we got up to ninety.

She had a favorite proverb, and if you were lucky enough to tell that one, she gave you a special smile: "If wisdom's way you wisely seek, five things observe with care: of whom you speak, to whom you speak, and how and when and where."

She was as lovely to look at as she was to have as a teacher. She had reddish hair, which she also wore with a fringe across the forehead, and lovely skin, with that flush associated with tuberculosis. She had to leave school at Christmas the second year, and died shortly after.

The teacher who took her place was Celia Adams. She was the sister of Lucy and Sarah Adams, the famous Vineyard-born midgets who used to travel with Barnum's Circus. The midgets, incidentally, were accomplished musicians. They gave performances in the town hall in the old days — but never on Sundays, for they were very religious. I think they were bridesmaids at Tom Thumb's wedding. When they retired, they returned to their home on the South Road just over the West Tisbury line in Chilmark. They gave teas, and afterwards entertained people by spinning wool on an old-fashioned wheel. Much of the furniture in the house — chairs, tables, beds — was miniature size, constructed especially for them.

Celia Adams was not a midget, but she was small, barely five feet. She was exceedingly intelligent and a good teacher. One afternoon when I was kept after school, she lined up two boys and birched them both, with emphasis, right in front of me. I was surprised. They were nearly as big as she was. I don't remember ever being birched myself, but managed to incur just about all the other punishments in the book. Once I was put in the corner with my dustcloth over my mouth and my hands tied behind me.

The worst of all, though, was when a girl in Mrs. Dunham's room told a lie and was discovered. We all felt that a serious crime had been committed and were horrified. It was as if someone had died. . . .

The grammar teacher in the room was a man who had been on the school committee for many years and was also principal of all the school. His name was Mr. Tilton. He was a learned man, but had a brutal nature and used methods that were questionable, to say the least. Someone asked him once how he dealt with a boy who didn't behave. "Well," he said, "when he's sitting at his desk, I take his head and I bend it back until it cracks!" Father was much opposed to him and used his influence to have him removed as principal.

In 1894 we went to Boston for a year. Father had just opened an office there, and took a house for us. But we were sick a good deal of the time. Finally Father said, "Go back to the Vineyard where you're healthy." Which we did. When we returned we learned that Mr. Tilton had become the school principal again. The pupils in his school were scared to death of him.

Mr. Tilton liked to talk. He would begin after the prayer — we always at school had a Scripture reading and then said the Lord's Prayer — and he would talk about various things and keep on talking maybe until recess! My sister Nina became very impatient with him, for she was eager to learn. She was a real scholar, the smartest one in the family. She spoke to Father about it, and Father advised her: "You just keep account of the run of the talk, put down the date and how long." Nina did. She also talked to the other children and got them all excited about it, and they circulated a petition to have Mr. Tilton removed. Someone told him one evening of what was going on. The next morning he got up before the class in all his majesty — he was a big man — and said he had heard about some petition being circulated to ask for his severance from the school. He had everyone stand, and then said that all those who were satisfied with his teaching were to sit down. Nina said they began to drop around her one by one. Finally there were only Nina and one boy still standing. The boy's name was Harry Walker, and his father was one of the two Democrats in the village. Mr. Tilton turned to Harry and said, "You're not satisfied? Such a terrible boy!" And Harry sat down. There was only Nina left. Mr. Tilton knew very well it was Father who had got him out once, and when he turned and spoke to Nina, his voice was full of animosity. "So it's you, is it?" he said. Nina said, "Yes, it is I." "Well, why aren't you satisfied?" he asked. She took out her piece of paper and read of the times of his long-winded talks. Then she picked up her books and walked out and never went back. She was tutored the rest of the year. After that she went to boarding school.

Mr. Tilton stayed on. I went to school to him as had Mary and Ruth as well. He never took Nina's doings out on me, and he liked Mary because Mary was a gentle soul. And he did one thing for which I've always been grateful. He had us learn a number of the *Psalms* by heart, and that chapter of *Ecclesiastes* that begins: "Remember now thy Creator in the days of thy youth..."

The next year I had Mr. Winter, a good teacher, and the year after that Mr. Fales. Mr. Fales was an excellent teacher, but he had a very hot temper. I remember what he did to Norman Benson — Norman is the only one left that entered school the year I did. He lives up at Lambert's Cove and has written his memoirs. Norman irritated Mr. Fales, and Mr. Fales pushed him down the stairs. We heard Norman's head go thump, thump, thump. The girls began to cry. The next day Norman's mother and father appeared, and Mr. Fales had to apologize to them. You could scarcely blame him, though, for as a youngster Norman was irritating beyond words. I suppose I was also rather irritating. It was so hard for me to sit still! I was always cutting up. Mr. Fales took me in the coatroom once and said to me: "You're the most impudent student, boy or girl, I've ever had in any school I've ever taught!" But I got very good grades, and I thought so long as I was getting good grades, that was it. But I promised to try and behave. Years later, in Boston, Father and a young lawyer who was doing some work for him went into a restaurant and sat down at a table where there was another man sitting. Before long it was discovered that it was Mr. Fales, my old grammar room teacher. They got to talking and eventually Mr. Fales asked Father: "Whatever became of your daughter Gratia, Cap'n Eldridge?" As it happened, I was at that time at Bloomingdale Hospital, doing recreation work with the mentally ill. When Father said I was at Bloomingdale, Mr. Fales grunted, "Hmph, about what I figured." "She's on the staff there," Father explained. After Mr. Fales left, the young lawyer protested to Father, "What a terrible thing to say about your daughter!" Father replied: "That's all right. He suffered plenty at her hands."

RUTH: For most children school was a compulsory treadmill. There were a few of us, though, who really did enjoy books and learning. My oldest sister Nina was one of them.

When she was in the final year of the grammar room, Father and Mother began to ponder over the problem of getting their brainy child more education. Sending her away to school was very expensive, and there were three others of us coming along after Nina. Though we were not in Nina's class, they felt we were worthy of some kind of education beyond grammar school.

Edgartown had just set up a high school, and Father and Mother decided that the solution to the problem was for the Town of Tisbury to do the same. Well, before the time for town meeting, Father got busy and secured estimates from Will Manter, H. N. Hinckley, and several other builders on the cost of adding another room upstairs next to the grammar room to serve as the high school. The estimate was $1,500. Then Father got the required number of signatures — mostly from fathers of our contemporaries — to put an article in the warrant for the appropriation of $1,500 to construct the high school.

The day of the town meeting came. At the end of the afternoon session we saw Father come up the street, and by the way he walked we feared the worst, for he looked good and mad. We ran to meet him, shouting, "Are we going to have our high school?"

"No, you're not going to have your high school," he said.

Crestfallen, we followed him into the house, where Mother was waiting. Women, of course, could not attend town meeting, because at this time they did not yet have the vote. Father threw his coat down on a chair in great disgust. In as calm a voice as she could muster Mother said: "Was it voted down, George? What were the objections?"

"Oh, you might know," Father replied. "First, the cost. It would raise their damn taxes. Second, *they* didn't have any high school, so why should their children? Third, they would have to get an off-Islander to teach, and how did they know what she would teach? You can't trust an off-Islander, you know. That pretty well cinched it. Somebody yelled, 'Question!' and the vote was taken, and only two voted for it besides me."

"You mean the fathers that signed the petition didn't vote for it?"

"No, Sydna, they didn't. Just Dr. Lane and E. T. Walker."

Nina let out a groan. "I guess we won't have a high school then."

"Yes," Mother said, "we will. We'll have it, and, I think, next year. I'll get to work on the women."

And it happened just as Mother said. I don't know how Mother did it. I only know that women held her wisdom in great respect and that when she had a conviction regarding an issue she presented her logic in such a tactful way that friend and foe alike came to agree with her.

GRATIA: In the fall of 1899 I went into the high school, very excited at the prospect of studying Latin. By studying Caesar, Cicero, and Ovid, too, I felt we were really getting connected with the world. I took four years of Latin and was never sorry. I got so I could read it at sight. I did wonder why they gave us Caesar before Cicero; it seemed to me Cicero was much easier.

In addition to Latin, I had two years of French, two of German, ancient history, European history, American history, English, Algebra, Geometry, Physics, Chemistry, and Bookkeeping. The only thing taught I didn't take was Geography. I loved high school and enjoyed studying all these things.

As usual, however, I was not too well behaved.

My first year in high school, the second and third as well, we had only one teacher, and because she had to teach every period, she didn't teach anything very well. In junior year we got fed up with it. We felt the town was not poor and could afford more teachers for the high school. So one day we went on strike. We paraded up and down Main Street. I think there were twelve, perhaps as many as fifteen, of us. There weren't many more in the high school altogether. During my four years there we were never more than twenty-three. The townspeople asked us why we were parading. "We're parading for better teachers!" we said. Fortunately the father of one of the girls was on the school committee and understood the situation. In my senior year we had two teachers in the high school, one from Harvard and the other from Smith. There had always been somebody from Boston University or from Bates, neither of which was much good in those days. But now we had really good teachers.

I was out of school the next year. Ruth went to Cushing Academy. Since the family could not afford to send two of us away to school at the same time, I stayed home. We lived then in a big house on Main Street (which we called Bonnie Castle), where Havenside now stands.

We had a number of troubles that year. A dear old aunt had taken in a schoolteacher as a boarder. When the weather got cold, the old aunt decided to go to Boston and asked Mother to take on her boarder for her until she returned to the Vineyard in the spring. Mother, being Mother, said she would. Unfortunately, Mother's brother died, and since he had named Mother executor, she had to go out to Wyoming to settle his estate, and the schoolteacher boarder was left in Mary's and my hands. We had to crawl out of bed much earlier than we liked to get our boarder off to school. Every morning we gave her Aunt Jemina's pancakes. Mary became a whiz at making coffee and pancakes in record time.

Then there was the furnace. It was an old, hot-air furnace. Every morning Mary would go down to look at it, and I would call down the register, "Is it out?" Back would come the reply, "Y-e-e-s!" After many despairing interchanges of this sort, we discovered our trouble was that we had been too stingy in banking the fire with coal the night before.

III
After School

GRATIA: When we were growing up you never heard anyone complaining of having nothing to do. We found plenty to do. In the first place, we played a lot at school. In the primary school part of the yard there were a number of posts the boys used to leapfrog over. It was a constant frustration to me that I couldn't leapfrog too because of my petticoats. After school we played "sailo" in the big yard. Someone was "it" and tried to catch us as we ran back and forth between the schoolhouse and the sidewalk on Centre Street. If you were caught you became a catcher also, and the game continued until all were caught. The first one caught was always "it" in the next game. We played "sailo" by the hour.

In winter we did a lot of coasting. We used to coast down Church Street and Spring Street. This was before there were any automobiles around; horses were never much of a hazard. Our favorite place to coast was over in the Company Field bordering Causeway Road. Beyond the cemetery at the top of the hill was what we called "cat hollow." On one side it went down precipitously into a little valley or hollow, then up a less precipitous hill on the other side. The boys used to make double-runners — two sleds placed one in front of the other and connected with a board. A boy would sit in front and steer, a girl or two girls would sit behind him, and another boy stood behind to get it going with a shove. It was a breathtaking descent. You sledded down the steep hill pretty fast, and the momentum carried you pretty much up the smaller hill opposite. Then you turned around and sledded down that hill — a little dividend. The double-runner was usually steered by ropes attached to the crosspiece in front. One boy who was more privileged than the rest, known then as Shug (later Colonel Roth), appeared on the hill, much to everyone's excitement, with a double-runner that steered with a wheel. He was a beau of Mary's, and he permitted her, at her urgent request, to steer his double-runner down the hill. No other girl in the history of the town had ever steered a double-runner down that hill.

Then there was skating. If there had been only a few nights of freezing weather, we used Ben Luce's Pond on the other side of the old Marine Hospital. With a few more such nights, we could go to Mink Meadows. In those days the pond was surrounded by tall trees and was a charming spot. After school we would walk the mile and a half down there, skate, then walk a mile and a half home. Sometimes on Saturdays we skated in the afternoon and again in the evening. Nobody had cars. Everybody walked.

When there was a still longer spell of very cold weather, we were able to skate at Tashmoo! This was before the big inlet was dredged, and the water was almost fresh, so the ice was sound. We would walk to the east bank, then skate across to Sarah Drew's Cove. Mia Farrow owns the land there now, I believe. We had a gorgeous time skating there. We had iceboats, too. They were nothing but wooden triangles with steering gear and a big sail. You had to hold on so tight that your gloves or mittens froze to the frame. It was exciting, though, and afterwards we would build a fire and get warm again. We played crack-the-whip and cross tag. My skates were the clamp kind and were always coming off. But I learned to skate backwards, go in a circle, and do the outer edge. We had a happy, jolly time. We skated a lot because often there wasn't much snow. I haven't skated since the thirties. I brought my skates home with me when I retired. I thought I'd skate, but I never did.

RUTH: "Now girls," Mother said, "if you have your lessons done, you can go over to Hursells and help tie tags."

The Hursells were a poor family across the street. The father had been a highly respected citizen, a carpenter by trade, but in his middle thirties he followed his brothers and sisters to the old cemetery, like them a victim of consumption.

Mrs. Hursell, her daughter Gertrude, aged ten, and son Henry, aged eight, had the house and the small plot of land it was on. The house was free and clear because Mr. Hursell had built it himself. There was a good-sized woodshed, which had served as a workshop for Mr. Hursell as well as a wood storage place, and his workbench still stood with his tool chest underneath. It also contained the outside tools, rake, spade, and hoe, and a bag of grain for the hens. The hen yard was back of the shed alongside the privy. There was a vegetable garden at the rear with a pig-nose apple tree in the middle, and the front of the house was a tiny lawn. The Hursells had a home, to be sure, but to feed, clothe, and keep the family warm was a struggle against head wind and head tide. There was Mrs. Hursell's mother to take care of besides.

Mrs. Hursell didn't know the meaning of leisure time. When she wasn't keeping house, cooking, or doing the usual motherly things, she was hard at work at what in those days was a flourishing home industry, especially in Vineyard Haven. There was an agent who received skeins of wool and different patterns for making babies' garments and robes and shawls and things of that nature to be sold in the retail stores. The wool and the patterns were parceled out among village women who had ability with a crochet hook and were in need of money. Mrs. Hursell was one of these women. You never saw her in her rocker by the window without a clean towel in her lap and some wool garment in the making.

A sideline of this business was tag tying. Garments that were to be sold had to have a price tag, and tag tying was putting a string through a little hole in the tag so that it would be ready for use. This was something children could do. At the Hursells' there were always piles and piles of the little white tags and bunches of pink strings. We girls would go over and sit around the tea table and tie tags by the light of the kerosene lamp. The mother would be busy with her crochet hook, the old grandmother would be dozing beside the stove. It always gave us a warm feeling because we knew they were happy to have us there, and we did our best to be gay and chatty. I guess we were silly, too, but it was such fun, everybody laughing, especially when somebody started to hiccough — then we'd hoot!

At the time I'm thinking of Henry was ten. He was small for his age and skinny, freckles all over his face and his hair a mass of tight curls. But Henry had the natural ability with tools his father had, and when our sled or some little thing in the house needed fixing, Mother would say, "Go and get Henry. He'll know how to fix it." And usually he did.

Henry's big responsibility was to keep the family warm through the winter. The cost of coal for the kitchen stove was prohibitive, and Henry had to keep a good supply of wood on hand. Some he got from Mr. Peakes's sawmill, which was a blessing, since Henry was too small to cut the logs. Mrs. Peakes gave him a wheelbarrow load in exchange for some of the grandmother's hulled corn. Henry was always hoping for a good northeaster, because then he could go around and collect fallen branches and cart them home for kindling.

Henry also helped the family with his hens. He sold some of the eggs, and at times when there wasn't going to be very much for Sunday dinner, he would appear in the kitchen with an old hen all plucked and ready for roasting. We thought Henry was such a good name for him — because he was so good with the hens.

Once I visited Henry while he was feeding his hens. I asked him if ever a hen got away from him after he'd chopped off its head. "Only once," Henry said. "It was turrible to see that critter running around without its head on! It ran smack into a fence, and then, when it got clear of the fence, it run into the road and got under Mr. Crocker's horse that was going by. Gee! I can't think of nawthin' more turrible than to have your legs want to run somewhere and you don't have no head to tell you you're headed for trouble!"

I told Henry about our keeping hens when we lived down-the-Neck. Mother had been brought up on a farm and was used to having fresh eggs. She knew how to chop off the heads of chickens, too. One day when Father was in bed with his rheumatism, he told Mother he sure would like some nice, fresh chicken soup. Mother went out and caught an old rooster that wasn't any use any more and brought him to the chopping block. Somehow, after she made her chop, the old rooster got away from her, and before we knew it he flopped right through the kitchen door and made straight for Father's bedroom and settled down under the bed. I guess Father thought the rooster was going to get lively again and maybe fly up on his bed. He began yelling and shouting orders to us kids to get him out, get him out! Mother got a broom and calmly scooped up the poor old rooster and grabbed him by the legs. Father said, "Never mind about the soup, Sydna. I don't believe I want it. Give it to the children."

When I finished my story, Henry said, "And I betcha you kids didn't want that soup neither. That was turrible the way that happened!"

"Henry, you should not say 'turrible.' The word is terrible."

"Say, my Grandmother says turrible and so does my Ma and so shall I. Turrible sounds much more turribler than your old terrible. I may be hopeless but I'm not helpless like some folks around here. You better go along home 'fore I lose my temper. I've got a turrible pile of work to do."

I remember another time, the day before Thanksgiving. Henry appeared at our back door with three nice big turnips. As he passed them to Mother, he said: "These turnips are for your Thanksgiving dinner, Mrs. Eldridge. I grew them myself and last week I dug them after the frost came. You know it's the frost makes 'em sweet."

Mother took the turnips and said, "My goodness, Henry, how in the world do you know how to grow such fine vegetables?"

"Well, you see, I used to get sawdust from Mr. Peakes for my hen house, and when the hens got it all dirty, I swept the whole business up and put it in a pile outside the hen yard. Well sir, around that pile the weeds started to grow like sixty, so I sez to myself, say, if that stuff makes the weeds grow, I betcha it'll make my vegetables grow, too. Sure enough, I spread that dirty sawdust along the vegetable rows, and they grew just like the weeds. Well, good-bye all. Mother says 'Happy Thanksgiving to you.' "

"Happy Thanksgiving to you, too!" we all shouted.

Mother laid the turnips on the table and shook her head in wonder. "That child has the wisdom of an old man in that curly head of his."

IV
Grandfather, Father, and Sardines

GRATIA: Father came from Chatham. He was the eldest of five, four boys and a girl. There were two others, but they died at an early age.

Father's great-grandmother was an Indian. Her name was Dorcas Wixum, and she came from South Dennis. A great-uncle told me she had the blackest eyes and was the quickest moving person he had ever seen. I think she was properly married to great-great-grandfather, because Father remembered her. He was about nine when she died at 103. I remember visiting this great-uncle in his last illness. He looked at me and said, "Eldridge, Eldridge!" Then he looked at Nina. *"Indian!"* he said. Dorcas had six sons and six daughters, and I think it's likely that many of the Eldridges on Cape Cod are descended from those six sons.

[As Gratia relates later, the daughters grew up in a family that was deeply concerned about social distinctions, about who was acceptable and who was not. This did not prevent them from taking great pride in their Indian heritage. Much was made of it when I was growing up, and I recall feeling especially blessed and superior because of the Indian in me. But then one day I sat down and figured it out. After generational dilution, the amount of Indian blood coursing through my veins and arteries came to about 3.2 per cent. Like 3.2 per cent beer, that was hardly enough to matter. E.E.M.]

I remember seeing Grandfather only once, but that is a vivid memory. We had sailed over to Chatham to visit him. I was in the kitchen when he came through the door from the dining room. He filled the doorway. He had a big frame, very broad shoulders. His head was slightly sunk between his shoulders as the result of a bad fall aboard ship when he was young. He had a great mass of iron-gray hair atop his head, a large beard, and deep, deep black eyes beneath heavy brows. He said very little to us girls. Although he had had five children of his own, he clearly didn't know what to do with us and perhaps decided the best course was to leave us alone. Mother was also a puzzle to him. He couldn't understand anyone as unselfish and kind and gentle as Mother. His own wife was very self-centered. She went to bed when she was forty and stayed there until she died forty-one years later. Grandfather couldn't believe Mother was sincere. He called her "a whited sepulchre."

As a young man Grandfather had a reputation for his daring seamanship. Once at Duxbury, Massachusetts, during a fierce storm, while all other ships were either safely at anchor or hove to, in a sudden break in the spray-dense horizon to the eastward a schooner under sail could be seen making for the harbor. "What damn fool is that?" someone exclaimed. "Couldn't be anybody but George Eldridge," was the speedy reply.

More than half of Chatham was seafaring, and Grandfather was held in very high regard because of his charts. People referred to him as "Chart George." For his part Grandfather was very interested in what went on in the town and took an active part in town and also county affairs. He was a staunch Republican.

Grandfather was fond of music and played the violin. He played the violin in the Baptist Church for many years. Not that he was religious. He was, in fact, something of a heretic. He delighted in argument and would happily spend all afternoon by some storekeeper's potbellied stove disputing religion with his more orthodox-minded friends. He knew the Bible as well as any of them. He played in the church simply because he loved music. After he had played for the church a number of years, the church got a new organ. Grandfather followed the installation with intense interest. When it was completed, he sat down at the keyboard and — to test the action, he said — played "Yankee Doodle." One of the good church sisters happened by just as he was finishing the final bars and came up to him and said, "Cousin George, what be that hymn you were a-playing?"

"Why, cousin," Grandfather replied, "don't you recognize 'Old Hundred'?"

"Ah, of course," she said, "I thought it sounded familiar. But, Cousin George, don't you think you had it a wee bit fast?"

Many years later I visited Chatham and by chance met a man who had known Grandfather. He offered to show me the old house. Other people were now living there, but there was a plaque on it in Grandfather's memory. As we walked by the side of the house, the man pointed out where Grandfather grew his cucumbers. "Cucumbers?" I said. "I didn't know he was also a gardener."

"Oh, he wasn't," the man said, "but he was passionately fond of cucumbers. He grew all kinds here."

I laughed until the tears came. I, too, am passionately fond of cucumbers. When I was young they called me "Cucumber Gratia."

When he was still very young, Father went to sea. He was only nine, in fact, the summer Grandfather installed him as cook aboard his schooner. Once they were anchored in Vineyard Haven Harbor and Grandfather was ashore visiting—he was an inveterate socializer. When it got later and later and Grandfather didn't return, Father decided he should start some pancakes for supper. He suffered terribly from seasickness, and he was bone tired. He put the dough on the griddle and then lay down, intending it to be only a minute or two. The next thing he knew Grandfather was there, the cabin full of smoke, the pancakes cinders.

In spite of the seasickness Father continued to go to sea. In winter he was in school. After he finished school he was with a ship fishing off George's Banks. The men would go out from the ship in dories, fish from the dories, and then return to the ship at the end of the day. On one occasion the mother ship signaled the dories to return because a storm was brewing. As they started for the ship, Father saw that one of the dories was having difficulty. Furthermore, he saw that the man in it was a young man who was on the Banks for the first time. Father turned around and went to help him. By the time he reached him, however, the sea had become very rough, and despite their combined efforts, both in one dory and trying to tow the other, they lost sight of the mother ship. The young man fell on his knees and began to pray fervently.

"Get off your knees and bail or I'll throw you overboard!" Father yelled at him. The young man could tell from the sound of Father's voice that he meant it, and he at once set to bailing. They were on the storm-ravaged sea all night and part of the next day before they were rescued by one of the other ships on the Banks.

On another occasion during a storm the captain went out of his mind and had to be restrained in his cabin. Father said the ship pitched and tossed so violently it took nearly all one's strength just to hang on. When they finally got back to Chatham, Father swore he'd never go to sea again. And he never did.

Father met Mother while on his trip seeing the world. It's difficult to imagine the Middle West being adventurous today, but in those days it was. He landed in Fort Wayne, Indiana. Mother was teaching school there. She was from Ohio originally. Father played the guitar, and with the idea of making some pocket money he went into a music store to ask if there might be somebody interested in taking guitar lessons. Also he was looking for a place to stay. As it happened, Mother's uncle, with whom she was staying, was in the store and overheard Father's inquiry about a place to stay.

"We take boarders, sir," the uncle said. "Would you care to come home with us?"

"Indeed I would, sir," Father replied.

Next day, as Father was having lunch, Mother came in rather late. A dressmaker was doing some work for her in an adjoining room and called to Mother for instructions and Mother called them back. Father thought it was ill-mannered for a young lady to participate in this kind of shouting match while she was having her meal, especially in the presence of a stranger, namely, himself. She paid no attention to him whatever, and he was very annoyed.

Well, they fell in love and became engaged and planned to marry the following spring.

Meanwhile Father returned to the Vineyard. In the fall of that year he was playing croquet, and for some reason or other the game was being played with iron balls. One of the them hit Father in the ankle and broke it.The doctor said he would never walk again without crutches or a cane — an overpessimistic prediction, but Father didn't know that then. He wrote Mother: "I know you don't want to marry a cripple, and therefore I won't hold you to your promise." Mother wrote back and said she wasn't that kind of person and that so far as she was concerned the engagement was still on. She was home in Bridgeville, Ohio, then, a small town near Zanesville. She had given up her position at the school. Her family was a farming family, and they were all excited about this Easterner coming to marry their Sydna. Two sisters were home then as well as Mother. They were all looking out the window when Father's carriage arrived. When he got out and they saw him walking with two canes, one of the sisters turned to Mother and said, "Oh, Syddie, is *that* your man? How could you!"

They were married in the sitting room. There was a love seat they sat on. They stood for the ceremony and then sat down again. Next day they took the train from Zanesville to Baltimore, and at Baltimore they took a boat to Boston. After the hot, dusty train Mother thought how delightful the boat was and the clean, cool sea air. In a very short time she was sick as a dog and didn't think the boat nice at all.

At the Vineyard, of course, Mother was a complete alien. People did not accept her, and she had a very lonely time at first. On the other hand, she was shocked by Vineyard mores. The coasting schooners might lie at anchor two weeks or more waiting for a fair wind. Sailors came ashore, and there was a good deal of immorality, especially down-the-Neck, where she and Father lived, away from things. Mother said there was only one woman she knew at the time who was respectable. All the others had immoral pasts. Children were born in wedlock, all right, but the thing was their fathers were not the husbands of their mothers. Some new blood got introduced into the town that way.

After Father quit the sea he went to work for Grandfather selling the latter's charts and coast pilot books. He was a good salesman and did so well financially that by the time he married Mother he was able to buy the house down-the-Neck and the chandlery and set himself up in the chandlery business. He did well at that also — for fifteen years. Then, I don't know what possessed Father. He was a restless person, of course, always thinking up new ideas, new schemes for this and that. Perhaps vanity had some-thing to do with it as well. One can only guess at this point. In any case, Father decided to go into the harness business. Vineyard Haven had a harness factory, the Crocker Har-ness Company, which was where the Martha's Vineyard

National Bank is now.   Mr. Crocker, the owner, came
to Father one day and said to him: "Captain Eldridge, you
have been a highly respected businessman in the eyes of
the villagers since you've been here and I've decided you
are just the man I've been looking for to run my harness
company."

Father must have been flattered. The harness company
was the biggest business in the village by far, employing
thirty or forty people. Mr. Crocker's offer must have
seemed very attractive. Father accepted. He sold the chandlery, invested heavily in the company, and became the
company's president. It wasn't long before Father discovered the real reason Mr. Crocker had recruited him. The
company was in serious financial difficulty, and things
went rapidly from bad to worse. Father felt he could save
the company if he could get ten good men to join him in
straightening out the company's affairs. He could find only
one man willing, Moses Vincent. Whenever he saw Moses
on the street, Moses would hold up ten fingers encourag-
ingly. But it was no use. When Father realized he could do
nothing, he resigned. Mr. Crocker found another man to be
president, an honorable man, a retired sea captain, but the
company went to pieces.

Father was with the harness company a little over a year.
The experience cost him not only a great deal of money but
his livelihood as well. He still had a wife and four young
daughters to support, and he was approaching fifty. He
had to think of something to do right away. After his years
working with Grandfather, he knew a great deal about
charts. The thing for him to do, he decided, was to go to
Boston and get into the chart publishing business. Which
he did.

People often ask: "But weren't there government charts?" Indeed there were, and they were pretty things to look at—in your living room with the aid of a magnifying glass. Father had been to sea, and he knew the way it was. Lumber schooner captains coming down from Maine, trying to feel their way through Pollock Rip against a stiff head wind, ship pitching every which way, water rolling off their oilskins onto the chart, they needed something they could *read*. The distinguishing feature of an Eldridge chart, of course, was its readability. The coastlines were shown with a heavy line, and soundings were in large, bold numerals.

Father had the charts printed, but the buoys had to be inked in by hand in red ink. That's where we girls came in. We did the hand work. Our attic on William Street was always full of charts waiting to be finished by hand. We had to make corrections also. Sometimes the government changed buoy positions and made other changes, and the charts had to be changed accordingly. A monthly bulletin came from Washington telling about the changes. Mary was past grand mistress at making corrections. She would skillfully scratch out the old position with a razor and put in the new one freehand. Ruth and I inked in the buoys. We used to spill the ink and do all kinds of things wrong. How we hated those charts!

But Mary did a lot of that work. She was paid seven cents an hour, we were paid five cents. We would far rather have had no money and no work. I had to put in two hours every Saturday morning before I was free for the day.

Father wanted us to be ahead with the charts so that orders could be filled as they came in. Sometimes we would be ahead, sometimes not. When the buoys and corrections were done, then we had to paste labels on the back with homemade paste to show what chart it was. They were lettered A through G. We would work far into the night on buoys and corrections, then get up early and paste the labels on the back. After that we had to roll them up and tie them — and they were great long things. I remember so well running down to the expressman with these great long rolls. The express office was next to where Brickman's is now. I'd come panting in, and the expressman would take them directly to the boat and get them on at the last possible moment, often without properly registering them, because he knew how important it was to get them off.

A sidelight of the chart story is an odd habit Ruth had. One of Father's ideas to make the charts more durable (at that time they were Grandfather's charts) was to have Mother bind the edges with cloth on her sewing machine. Father got this idea while Mother was carrying Ruth. After Ruth was born Mother had only to sew on her sewing machine and Ruth would promptly fall asleep. Ruth claimed she was marked for life by that sewing machine. Whenever she heard *any* sewing machine she had an irresistible urge to fall asleep.

In 1894, in addition to the charts, Father took over the publishing of the *Tidebook* as well. Although he was the one who developed the idea originally, Grandfather did the publishing because Grandfather had the established reputation.

RUTH: After the tide tables were all figured out and sent off to the printer for the next year's *Tidebook* there came a time of great excitement. Shortly before Christmas Father would come home and produce with a flourish a pile of cards that were the contracts for the advertising. We would listen entranced as he read them off to Mother: "Thames Tow Boat, full page, third year. Crosby Catboats, half page, fifth year. Briggs and Beckman, Sailmakers, half page, fourth year." And so on.

The high point was always the ship chandlers, for they made their payment in groceries rather than money, and although most of the things weren't especially tempting for girls who were always hungry — the potatoes, dried fish, pails of lard, bags of rice and dried beans — there were always good things like apples, which gave our cellar such a nice smell most of the winter. Sometimes there were even fancy things like chocolate drops.

One year when we were about to the bottom of the last barrel, there, between the layers of excelsior, all done up in white tissue paper, we found something different. "What is it? What is it?" we shouted eagerly as Mother undid the wrappings. It was a small flat can, and the label was written in some strange foreign language. "This, children," Mother said, "is nothing but a can of sardines. It's imported from Italy, to be sure, but the price — 45¢ — what was your father thinking of! Forty-five cents buys a bushel of potatoes! Well, we'll just have to wait until Father gets home from Boston to explain this!"

Father came home Saturday night, and after supper, as we sat around the table, Mother brought forth the can of sardines and said to Father in a coolish tone: "George, this was in the lot of *Tidebook* groceries. What made you get such an extravagant thing?"

Father replied with all the dignity he could muster. "Sydna," he began, "there is more to that can of sardines than you are aware of. It reaches into the realm of education for our daughters, and I know that's a thing dear to your heart. First, you see, there, right on the outside of the can, there is the example of the great Italian language, spoken by the people of Italy long before the day of the great Caesar. Is that not an impressive eye-opener to our island-born daughters? And speaking of opening, I think the time has now come to open the can." Father took out his pocket knife and unfolded the big blade.

"Would you like me to open it for you, George?" Mother offered. "'You know you're not very good at this sort of thing."

And indeed he wasn't. He was a superb sailor, he could charm the saints with his guitar playing, his head was always full of very clever ideas, but when it came to such practical matters as driving a nail or opening a tin can he was all thumbs. But he declined Mother's offer with an assured air. "I believe I can manage this, Sydna, thank you. You see, the can is flat and the metal is always fairly soft and thin." Of course the knife right away slipped and cut his finger and oil spurted out and ran down his sleeve. "All right, you open it!" he said peevishly, shoving the can toward Mother. "Just be quick about it so I can continue with my object lesson."

Mother took the can into the kitchen while Father wiped up the oil that had run down his arm to the elbow and sucked at his bleeding finger. In a trice Mother was back with the can neatly opened.

"Now, Sydna," Father proceeded, "the Bible, as you know, is full of references to the olive groves of Jerusalem, to Christ on the Mount of Olives, but what has that meant to our daughters with all their Sunday School learning? The oil in which these sardines are packed is from those very olive trees. Extracting the oil from the olives is a marvel in itself, and one is compelled to admire the great resourcefulness of the peasants for learning how to use nature's bounty and sharing it with us.

"Finally, we come to the sardines themselves. Observe the nicety with which the packer has tempted the purchaser. Each tiny fish lies next its neighbor in complete cooperation and adaptability. Quite an example to humans, I'd say. Our daughters know the codfish by sight, the mackerel, the herring, and even the squeteague and the hornpout, but never a sardine has swum in Vineyard waters or been caught in the trap of any local fisherman. Here then is a brand new species for them to consider."

As Father stopped to gather his thoughts, Mother said: "What do we do with these sardines, then? Considering all they represent in the world of education, it seems rather unappreciative of us just to eat them."

"Ah, Sydna, I am about to discuss this point if you will be patient. Two years ago, if you will recall, when the New York Yacht Club was in our harbor, your husband was invited aboard Mr. J. Pierpont Morgan's yacht *Corsair*. The time came when refreshments were in order, and a steward appeared, and Mr. Morgan asked me what I would like to drink. I replied that as I was a teetotaler I would have some ginger ale. Soon the steward returned with a tray of bottles and glasses, and on the tray was a plate of crackers, oblong affairs, and some sardines exactly of this variety. Mr. Morgan helped himself to a cracker and placed one of the sardines on that cracker neat as a pin. I watched carefully and was able to do the same. Last summer I was again a guest on the *Corsair*, and the whole episode was repeated, sardines, crackers, and all.

"Now, when I go to Boston, I intend to go to Mr. S.S. Pierce's fancy grocery store and get a box of those special crackers. I shall then show my daughters the correct way to place a sardine on one so that next summer, when Mr. Morgan invites me aboard his yacht, I will say to him, 'Mr. Morgan, I have four daughters and I would be pleased for them to see your beautiful yacht, if it would not be an intrusion.' He will probably say, 'Yes, indeed, Captain Eldridge, Mrs. Morgan and I will be delighted — say, at four o'clock.' That'll mean ginger ale, sardines, and crackers. The daughters will have been trained by my forethoughtfulness to conduct themselves with decorum and finesse, especially important when refreshments are served aboard the *Corsair*."

We girls were all ears like a donkey and spellbound with the whole idea.

"Well, George," Mother said matter-of-factly, "that being the case, perhaps those sardines were worth the forty-five cents, after all."

V

Playmates

GRATIA: Mother and Father were married three years before the first baby was born, and during that time Mother taught school. There was a branch of the public school for down-the-Neck children on Hatch Road then. Mother taught the primary grades there and also tutored some older boys. I believe she was an excellent teacher, for she was always very good at explaining things to us when we had difficulty with our homework.

Nina, the oldest, was born in October, 1878; two years and nine days later came Mary; in another two years there was Ruth; then, finally, once more in two years, I came along.

Nina took after Grandfather Eldridge, the one who originated the charts. He was a man without a formal education, but he had a brilliant and very creative mind. Nina was a scholar, and also enjoyed music very much. In temperament she was pessimistic — also like Grandfather.

I was always closest to Mary. Our tastes were more alike. Mary was awfully good — all her life her greatest desire was to be good. She was like Grandfather Saurbaugh, Mother's father, who was thoroughly good, a truly saintly person. He was a man of modest means, with a farm of only 500 acres. I believe he never managed to pay the mortgage, but when he died he had a funeral train said to be a mile-and-a-half long. Everyone loved him. Mary was born with that desire for goodness. She was always interested in spiritual things. As a child she could be very stubborn. Among other things, she never wanted to go to bed. One night Father said: "All right, let's let her stay up as long as she likes." She had a rocking chair, and she loved to rock. Everyone went to bed and left her rocking away. After a while Father got up and went and asked her if she wasn't ready to come to bed. "Ain't s'eepy a bit," she said. "Ain't s'eepy a bit!" And she went on rocking until finally she fell asleep in the chair. She was always mild and gentle in her manner, but as stubborn as anyone you ever met. Very reasonable, but so determined. The iron hand in the velvet glove.

Mother was prominent in the W.C.T.U., and sometimes went off-island on trips. She usually left the three of us — Nina was by then away at boarding school — in charge of a lady across the way, who came over and took care of us. Sometimes, however, she left Ruth and me at the mercy of Mary. Mary was terribly penurious. No matter how much Ruth and I teased her to get good things to eat, she steadfastly refused. She said to us: "Next week this time you won't know whether you had it or not."

Mary had a very nice disposition and never lost her temper. Nina had a quick temper. She was also generous and warmhearted. But Mary was just naturally easy to get along with, and always accommodating. She loved to skate, loved to play tennis. But she was never very strong. She was sick a good deal of her life. She was Father's favorite.

Nina, Mary, and I were dark in our complexions, but Ruth was fair. She had brown eyes and fair skin. We used to tell her she didn't belong to the family, that Mother and Father had adopted her from a captain off a ship. We knew perfectly well it wasn't true, but we liked to tell it to her to rile her up. Ruth was very pretty. She was the beauty of the family. She had dimples and very fetching ways about her. At an early age she had more beaux than any of the rest of us. When she was only ten, a boy fell desperately in love with her. "Oh, Ruthie, Ruthie!" he used to say, "stick to me and be my only wife!" He took her out for ice cream once. Since he had enough money for only one dish, he sat there and watched her eat it.

Ruth was artistic and creative. She was also willful. Mother said she was the most difficult of all to bring up because she was so willful. When I was six months old, Mother said, "Now that is a reasonable child." She always said I was easy for that reason. If I was naughty, I would say: "Yes, I did it! Give me my punishment and let me get it over with." But Ruth would never admit she was wrong. If she did anything wrong, it was somebody else's fault. But she was very, very generous.

In her teens Mary took violin lessons. She went to Boston and took lessons from Arthur Fiedler's father, then the first violinist of the Boston Symphony Orchestra. He thought she had a future as a violinist, and when he went back to Vienna, he wanted to take Mary with him. But she was more interested in religion than in the violin. In any case, I think the family would not have let her go. She was then only eighteen.

Mary taught Ruth to play the violin. What arguments *that* brought forth!

RUTH: Closely associated with our growing up was a boy who lived across the street. His name was Benjamin, but we always called him Bennie. He was Mary's age and in her class at school

Bennie was the only son of well-to-do parents, born late in their lives and cherished and protected in every way. He was a mannerly, thoughtful child, always full of ideas about how we could all have a good time together.

In spite of his parents' good care, Bennie came down with a severe attack of scarlet fever when he was fourteen. There had been no scarlet fever on the Vineyard for many years, and doctors were puzzled over how Bennie had got the germ. But get it he did, and he was a very sick lad. When the fever was gone and the quarantine was over, we saw him sitting out on his side steps. He looked so pale and thin. But when he stood up he looked as though he had grown a foot! He didn't look like our old playmate a bit.

Bennie kept growing taller and taller as the days passed, and more and more conspicuous among the boys and girls his age. He was terribly self-conscious about his growth, and began stooping to offset his height. I used to think it would have been better if Bennie was bowlegged, which he wasn't. Bennie was so averse to attracting attention to himself and being conspicuous that he decided not to try to change anything, to let Mother Nature have her way without any help from him. He kept on wearing short pants and keeping his voice where it was. He registered a sort of falsetto except when some joke took him by surprise and he would break into a hearty laugh. Then there came tumbling out a deep bass that would surprise us girls and make us want to laugh. Bennie, shocked by his lapse, would revert to his usual falsetto. We tried to help by not noticing things, but it was hard, because whenever we looked him in the face, he would think we were staring at the little tufts of whiskers that came bristling out more and more, and he would blush and turn away.

Bennie's parents were well aware of his adolescent problems and didn't really know what to do about them. They did the best they could to promote contact with other boys and girls. They provided Bennie with lots of games, which were a special source of pleasure to all of us. On Wednesday nights, when Mother went to prayer meeting, one of us would go over to Bennie's and ask him to come to our house and bring his tiddlywinks and lotto. Bennie always beat us, but we didn't care, for he was so comical and such great company.

There was usually a game of hopscotch drawn in chalk on the sidewalk by Bennie's gate. Bennie won at hopscotch too, partly because he had a very special stone that was flat and stayed put, partly because he never stepped on the lines. After hopscotch he would often offer a swing in his hammock. We always said yes, for Bennie did the swinging.

Mary, being the eldest of us three, had the first swing. She would have fifteen swings, nice and evenlike. Then I would seat myself in the hammock with an air of pleasant expectancy. This air of mine somehow aroused the spirit of competitiveness in Bennie. There would be several terrific swings, an abrupt full stop, and then a fancy twist of the wrist that made the hammock turn upside down. If Bennie dumped me out, my turn was over. Since I was not very good at hanging on upside down, my turn was always of short duration.

Then Gratia would spring into action. Gratia loved acrobatics and was interested in using the hammock for the purpose. But Bennie frowned on such liberties being taken with his hammock. As soon as Gratia finished off some fancy stunt, he would say with all dignity, "Now we'll go and play hopscotch."

Bennie had great respect and affection for Mary. They would often do their lessons together after supper, and Bennie sought her company in other ways. Then Mary took up the violin and had little time to spend with Bennie. She went to Boston for her lessons, which was time consuming. As well as an expense. To get his money's worth, Father decided that Mary should teach me what she learned from her Boston teacher. I'm ashamed to say that I never applied myself to the violin in exchange for Mary's patience. The only time I practiced was when Father was expected home on a weekend. When I heard the boat whistle Saturday afternoon, I would get out my violin and start practicing.

When Bennie heard Mary playing on her violin, he was fired with an ambition to learn to play too. His father immediately ordered a violin for him from Montgomery Ward. As soon as it arrived, Bennie brought it over in its shiny new case to show us.

"It's beautiful, Bennie," we told him.

"How about giving me lessons, Mary? he asked.

"I'll be glad to, Bennie. However, I'll have to charge you for the lessons."

"Of course," Bennie said. "How much?"

"Fifty cents an hour," Mary said.

Bennie had been brought up on Vineyard thrift. He thought fifty cents an hour was a little steep. He considered a few moments, then suggested, "How about half an hour for twenty-five cents?"

"No," Mary said, "I can't give any half-hour lessons."

I thought it was time for me to offer my services. "I'll give you half an hour's lesson," I said.

"Well," Bennie said, "Let's see now. Of course you're only half as good as Mary, so your price should be half her price. Half of fifty is twenty-five for the half hour if it was Mary, and half of twenty-five is twelve-and-a-half cents. Well, I'll give you thirteen cents."

And so once a week Bennie's front parlor was lighted up, and I went to give him a lesson.

When spring came with its long afternoons for out-of-door games, I resigned as Bennie's teacher. It wasn't just the lure of springtime fun. Bennie was a problem. He was shy and didn't feel comfortable having me take hold of his hands to show him how to finger the strings and hold the bow. When he saw me about to do this, he would back away. By the end of the lesson, he had backed away just as far as he could get, right into the corner of the room, where he couldn't possibly draw his bow if he wanted to.

Oh well, I was glad to call it quits. I did miss the thirteen cents, though.

GRATIA: I never wanted to go with the others. When Nina was home, Nina and Mary were together. When Nina was away, Ruth and Mary were together. It just happened that their friends matched them, and they were always together. I preferred not to go with them and was by myself a good deal.

I was never musical. Father was fanatically fond of music. Friends would come, and they were all musical. I had an uncle who was a musician, and he and his wife played duets. When they visited our house in the summer, Father made me sit absolutely still and listen. I couldn't even read! I wanted to smash the piano. I didn't know what it was all about. I don't know yet. Of course, I could never carry a tune, and I felt inferior because of it. "Shh, Gratia! Don't sing!" they'd say to me. It mortified me terribly.

But I was strong. I was a good tennis player. Ruth and I used to have fisticuffs. Once I had a fight with Nina. I don't remember what it was about. Mother said she was going to whip me. I picked her up and put her in the closet and shut the door on her! She laughed and laughed. She came out of the closet and said, "Gratia, I guess you're too old to be whipped!"

Once, when we were quite young, Ruth and I were playing with matches in our room on the third floor. The room had a low ceiling, and there was a line of clothes strung between two hooks. An errant breeze came in the window, the matches flared up, and the clothes caught afire. They were a flaming mass. Ruth grabbed the line and threw it on the floor, and we quickly stamped out the flames. But a beautiful dress of Ruth's was burned, and so was Mother's best silk. When Mother found out she said to Ruth: "Ruthie, since you're the older, I expect you were the leader in this. Gratia, go cut me a switch so I can whip Ruthie." I was tickled to death Ruth was going to get the whipping and not I, and I cut a good stout switch. But when

I returned with it, Mother said: "Why did you get such a big stick? While you've been gone I've been talking with Ruthie and I think you're just as much to blame as she is, so I'll have to whip you both." Of course Mother never liked to whip. In daytime, for punishment, she would send me to bed. That was terrible. I'd say to her: "Oh, don't send me to bed. Whip me instead and get it over with!" It was torture for me to hear other children playing outside and not be able to go out myself.

I got into a lot of scrapes. But Mother could always rely on my telling the truth about things. If she asked me, I would 'fess up. My conscience was proverbial in the family. For instance, we had a bicycle that had to be divided between the three of us — four of us when Nina was home from school. We each had our day when we were allowed to use it. It happened that one of us was needed to help out overnight with a mother and her children who lived down near the end of Herring Creek Road. I was elected to go and I felt it was unfair. To make it less unfair, I thought I should take the bicycle. So I took it and started out. Father said to Ruth: "Are you going to let Gratia go on the bicycle?" Ruth replied: "That's all right, she won't get far. Her conscience won't let her." Sure enough. I got to thinking about having the bicycle on a day that wasn't really mine. Before I reached the end of the street I turned around and went back. I even walked instead of using the bicycle, so conscience-stricken did I feel.

RUTH: Mr. Peakes lived next door with his little son Freddie. He supported the two of them by sawing wood with a power saw in his barn. The whine of that saw cutting through logs, stopping every now and then for a bad knot, was for years associated in my mind with autumn. It was then he would be getting ready for the winter trade.

I don't know exactly where he got the wood. Once I met him with his horse and wagon in Tashmoo woods on one of those old roads that never led anywhere except to somebody's wood lot. Perhaps he had an arrangement with the lot owner, a certain amount of cut wood for the owner, a certain amount of wood Mr. Peakes would sell to others. Or perhaps the owner had died and gone to Heaven, in which case who was to object to Mr. Peakes's taking the wood free for nothing?

Freddie's mother died when he was born, and Mr. Peakes did his best at bringing him up. But being a man, what could you expect? Freddie's nose was forever on the run, and there was only a red bandana he kept in his pocket for weeks to cope with the flow. He was always having sore throats. He would forget to put on rubbers and his coat. He was always appearing with an old sock around his neck. He had bilious spells and always a peculiar sour smell after he'd been sick. Freddie loved pies and cakes, and there would usually be the remains of one or the other on the kitchen table. They never really tempted any of us, though, because there were so many flies buzzing around.

If we didn't see Freddie around for a day or so, we said, "Guess Freddie's sick again." Then Mother would make some gruel and take it over to him. We went along and took with us the book that was Freddie's passion: *With H. M. Stanley in Darkest Africa*. He would look at the pictures by the hour — great snakes, crocodiles, lions, and elephants. They made him forget his stomachache. Or so he said.

Mother thought Freddie should go to Sunday School. So on Sunday mornings he would come over with a clean shirt on and his hair plastered down wet as a sop and the part all lopsided. Mother would take one look and say, "Freddie, dear, I think you'd better take off that nice clean shirt and let the girls help you wash up at the sink a bit."

Freddie, always cooperative, would peel off his shirt, and whichever of us was ready for Sunday School would start scrubbing, just the face, neck, and ears, the rest didn't show. We couldn't have done anything about the rest of him. In the first place, we couldn't manage that at the sink, and, in the second place, we wouldn't dare, boys being different from girls.

Well, the church bell would be ringing just as Freddie was getting back into his shirt, and down the street we'd hurry, we girls and our little neighbor Freddie skipping along ahead of us, happy as could be, his face so clean and shiny, we girls all aglow with our big sisterly ministrations.

VI
Rules and Duties

GRATIA: We didn't do many things together as a family because Father was away a good deal of the time. He was home on weekends only. But one weekend Father decided we should all sail over to Chatham and visit his parents. Poor Nina! She had to lie on a mattress in the cabin the whole time because she was so seasick. But we younger ones weren't affected. I remember we got the most extraordinary tan. It was the color of copper. I've never had anything like it before or since. It was a misty sort of day, and somehow that gave us the copper color. Toward evening the wind died down, and we drifted and drifted. Father said: "We won't make Chatham tonight. We'll have to anchor." Mother was afraid. She was a farmer's daughter, and knew nothing about the sea. We children weren't afraid. What was there to be afraid of? Wasn't Father with us, and, look, you could see lights on the shore not too far away. There was no reason to be afraid. Father fixed us a place to sleep in the furl of the sail. In the morning everything was sopping wet. But soon the sun rose and dried things out and a wind sprang up, and we proceeded merrily to Chatham.

Father was a complex man. He was so creative, so full of ideas, but he had his dark side too. When he came home from Boston we were always delighted to see him. He would sit down and tell us all his adventures, in great detail, of the plays he had seen. He was so good at it that it was almost as good as being there. We would hang on every word he said. I remember one play, *Private Secretary*, with William Gillette as the leading character. He played the part of a very impatient man. One of his lines was, "Where's zhurink?" said very quickly. ("Where is your ink?") It became one of our sayings. We used it all our lives. Where's zhurink? Where's zhurink?

But then something would happen, something would set Father off. He had a fearful temper. He would rage up. Just explode.

He was very strict. He had definite ideas about the way things should be. For instance, we had to go to bed at nine o'clock, even in our teens. We had to come straight home from school. We had to have permission to go out of the yard. He didn't like us to get good grades in school, for that meant we were spending too much time on school and not enough on other things. We were not permitted to bring homework from school. School was the place for learning and, according to Father, we spent enough time in school. At home we should be outdoors, or helping Mother. In the house each thing had a certain place, and woe betide anyone who let anything get out of place. We had a desk in the dining room, a sort of business desk, and nothing was ever to be left on top of that desk; this had to be clear at all times.

Once I had the misfortune to leave a book on top of that desk. This was a double offense, since the particular book was a schoolbook. It had a story in it we started in school, and I brought it home with me because I couldn't wait to see how it ended. I was upstairs when Father discovered the book. His voice, demanding to know who had done this forbidden thing, shook the house. I didn't even know I was the one, I simply felt an overwhelming sense of guilt. I scurried down the stairs as fast as my feet would carry me. I found Father standing in the middle of the room with his arms stiff at his sides and his head thrust forward, waiting for me. A quick glance at the desk told me I was indeed the culprit.

"Is this your schoolbook, Gratia?" he said.

"Yes, Papa."

"Did you leave it on the desk?"

"Yes, Papa."

"You remember the things I've told you?"

"Yes, Papa."

"Then why have you deliberately disobeyed me?" He began to shake, and his face got crimson. I suppose I was afraid he was going to beat me — although I can't remember that he ever disciplined any of us physically. It frightened me to look at him. At the same time I was afraid to stop looking at him. I was totally incapable of uttering a word.

Suddenly Father seized the book and threw it to the floor and stomped on it with both feet. At this point I fled to the kitchen to find Mother. Thankfully, I found her. I buried myself in her arms and cried and cried. After I had my cry

Mother quietly got up and went to find Father to try to calm him.

When his rampage was over, Father's anger would sub- side into a sour sulkiness. The sulkiness would last for days. It would cast the whole household into a state of gloom. When Father finally left to go back to Boston, we were happy to see him go — it was like a holiday. But then we were delighted to see him come home again.

He was very fond of us really. He often sent us presents. Mother had continually to contend with him over his ex- travagances. He used to send us dress lengths, material for making a dress. I remember a big package arriving with a dress length for each of us inside it. He had excellent taste too. Another time he sent me a beautiful plaid. It was a beautiful, bright dark blue with black, and the black had a kind of fur to it. It was an extraordinary material, I've never seen anything like it.

MARY: Father was of an artistic temperament. He was interested in drama and poetry and music. Mother had a practical nature. She was raised on a farm and was used to going to bed early and getting up early. In the first years of their marriage, before there were any children, Father would read to Mother in the evenings. There was a long poem he liked especially — Owen Meredith's *Lucile.* Mother said she learned how to sleep with her eyes open.

Father was always gentle with me. It was he who started me on the violin. "Music hath charms to soothe the savage beast, To soften rocks, or bend a knotted oak." He was so proud when I told him Arthur Fiedler had offered to take me back to Vienna with him to study.

"You'll surely go, won't you, Mary?" he said.

"I'll think about it, Papa." I told him.

But I knew right away I didn't want to go. I didn't want to make a life of the violin. I felt God had other plans for me. But I didn't know how to say this to Father. He had so many frustrations and disappointments. He was struggling so hard in Boston. No one properly appreciated his navigational ideas. I couldn't bear the thought of adding to his disappointment.

[Rummaging in our attic closet when I was ten I discovered an old violin case with a violin inside. I brought it down to Mother, and she acknowledged it was hers. It took her a while to string it and rosin the bow to her liking. Finally she tuned it to the piano and tried some scales. Up and down she went like the wind, without a miss, it seemed to me. "I'm terribly out of practice," she said. She read with ease anything I put in front of her, no matter how many sharps or flats. I was astonished. In the months that followed Mother played a number of times, but only when someone specifically asked her to do so. She was preoccupied with her church work. Within the year the violin found its way back into the closet, and I never heard Mother play again. E.E.M.]

GRATIA: I think Mother distributed her attentions fairly. They say I, being the youngest, got more attention, but I don't think that was the case. As I mentioned before, I was independent and never wanted to trail after my sisters. Mother never believed in having the older ones look after the younger ones — except in special situations. So that wasn't a problem.

We all liked to cook. I made the family bread and baked the beans every Saturday. I used molasses and bacon or butter, not salt pork, because Father thought it was not good for digestion. His family had had a bad time with indigestion. We had to make our chowders without salt pork. We were not allowed to have pie very often, and doughnuts never. This in a New England household!

The main thing I remember about breakfast is fried potatoes. We always had fried potatoes. We had eggs and cocoa, too, and oatmeal. Saturday night we had beans and piccalilli, and on Sunday morning we had beans again. We ate a good deal of fish, which was cheap and good and fresh, and we had clams. A family came by the house with clams in a milk can and ladled out what we wanted. Turnips and cabbage were staples. Mother fixed what she called "hot slaw," sliced cabbage done in a spider and very good. We bought our meat from a meat cart that came around. Lamb's liver was ten cents a pound, steak was twenty-eight cents. Father insisted on graham bread. We never had white bread at home. When we went to someone else's house and had white bread, it was a big treat for us. Drinking water with meals was taboo. Father contended that you didn't chew your food properly if you drank water while you were eating. To this day I never serve water at my table. Father had a book by a Dr. Hall on health, and he practiced Dr. Hall's ideas on us girls. Health was a big concern to him, since he had suffered a good deal of ill health. He was long troubled with rheumatism. To ward off its effects, he always carried an Irish potato in his pocket, a white potato. He carried it until it was nearly fossilized. He delighted in taking it out of his pocket and having people guess what it was.

Then there was cleanliness. Father greatly admired a restaurant-owner friend in Boston who required his waitresses to bathe every day. That was most unusual in those days. We bathed once a week. We had a big, tin-lined tub in the kitchen. All week long it stood upended out of the way. On Saturday nights we took it down and had our baths right there in the kitchen. We got the water warm in the washboiler on the cookstove. Vineyard Haven, being a clean place, we really didn't get very dirty. I remember how unfair I thought it was that Ruthie with her pink white skin, washed and washed and always looked clean no matter what, whereas I, who had sallow skin, washed and washed and somehow never looked clean.

In our teens we all had our duties Saturday mornings. I had to mop the kitchen floor, clean down the front and back stairways, and bake the beans. Mary loved to iron. She liked to see the results of her handiwork, coming out all nice and smooth and dainty. It wasn't her way of avoiding more arduous tasks. Mary never avoided anything. But it was Mary's and Ruth's job to clean the living room and dining room. The trouble was they used to get into great disputes over what was important. Ruth wasn't interested in cleaning, and Mary was a desperate cleaner. Ruth liked to fix things pretty. Ruth loved flowers.

RUTH: The distinguished house on our street belonged to a successful whaling master, Captain Richard Luce. I don't remember him at all. He died before we moved to William Street. It was his widow and her garden I recall so vividly.

The house was one of the largest and finest in town. For some reason Captain Luce elected to build his house, not on the harbor front, as most retiring captains had done, but on our street, some distance from the water. Perhaps he'd had his fill of looking at the sea, or perhaps his wife prevailed upon him to put the house where she could forget the sea and the years of loneliness and fearfulness it had caused her during her husband's long absences. There was a widow's walk at the top of the house, however, and from here the captain could train his spyglass on the harbor. He knew when a ship was setting sail for foreign seas, and it was said Captain Luce was always at his glass to wish departing neighbors Godspeed.

The Luce property extended right through from William Street to Spring Street. The house was long and narrow, extending two-thirds the depth of the property. The main entrance was on William Street, and an ornamental fence, breast high, curving with a graceful sweep up to the front door, created an atmosphere of genial hospitality. There was a spacious veranda on the eastern side, where one could sit and enjoy the beautiful lawn with its wine-glass elms. On the western side was the garden, in constant view of many of the rooms. Double glass doors from the dining room gave access to the path that led to the garden gate.

The garden was designed to conform to the narrow, oblong proportions of the house. In the center was a double, circular row of boxwood, like a maze in Old World gardens. Here tea roses grew, sheltered and protected like royal children in the inner court of a palace where their beauty and culture could not be contaminated by those less royal. The space between the boxwood circles served as a walk, and on the outside were the sturdy perennials — phlox, iris, foxglove, chrysanthemums — all blooming when their time came to give a continuous color contrast with the boxwood's dark green. A thick hedge of flowering shrubs and choice evergreens surrounded the garden, to protect the plants from devastating northeasters.

Screening the garden from the street was a border of lilacs, purple and white, syringa, and old-fashioned privet with its overpowering fragrance. Great bushes of Japanese quince terminated the border of shrubs at either end with their breathtaking blazes of crimson blossoms. There was a tiny bank between the shrubs and the fence; this was covered with myrtle. Such a wealth of heavenly blue was mine as I reached through the fence for flowers to fill my May baskets!

Once, just after I had finished picking a nice big bunch of myrtle, I heard a sound in the garden, and suddenly there was the widow Luce in her long black duster, basket on her arm, busy with pruning shears on the other side of the hedge. I saw that she saw me, and I rose to my feet and held up the bouquet of stolen myrtle. "See, Mrs. Luce," I said, "I needed some flowers for my May basket, and we don't have any flowers except dandelions. Wouldn't you like me to pick another bunch for you?"

"That's all right, child," she said. "No, you needn't pick any more for me. When you pick again, however, please be careful not to pull up the roots."

"No, Mrs. Luce, I will — I mean yes, Mrs. Luce, I won't!" I went home after that, fast as anything.

I remember the widow Luce in her garden again on a late summer afternoon. She was showing her treasures to a visitor. So exquisite she looked, with her tiny black lace cap atop her white curls and a lace shawl over her shoulders. Her hands were so dainty as she pointed with dignity and pride to certain special blossoms, like her children on parade in their Sunday best.

The widow Luce was not a sociable person by town standards. She was content to live alone in her big house with just a housekeeper companion. We saw her only in her garden surrounded by her "children," tending them with care and understanding, and occasionally giving them a disciplining snip with the pruning shears.

The heart and mind of a child are often touched by intangible things, things that cannot be wholly grasped or explained. As I made my way to school each day, I would glimpse a flash of color from the garden, catch the fragrance from the flowers, see the old lady attending her simple needs in a leisurely manner, at peace with herself and the world around her. I felt a fullness in my heart and the overwhelming desire to sing.

VII
Jaunts

GRATIA: Unless you had lots of relations there wasn't much going to dinner at other people's houses on the Vineyard, a fact rather distressing to Mother. She had grown up in the Middle West, where people were open-handed and hospitality was the rule. There were, however, two places we did go. One was a place on the Edgartown Road. Aunty Sally, as we used to call her, like Mother, had been raised in the Middle West and was accustomed to entertaining. We went to Aunt Sally's a number of times. Unfortunately, it was rather far away — two miles from Edgartown meant about five from Vineyard Haven. I remember once Mother hired a liveryman to take us a dollar-and-a-half's worth toward Edgartown. He took us up the road a distance and then let us off. I don't know how far it was, but it was surely several miles short of Aunt Sally's. The picture is still vividly in my mind, Mother striding resolutely ahead, we girls trudging behind, hot and hungry and bitterly complaining.

The other place we used to go was Aunt Lottie Beetle's. She was married to Uncle Henry Beetle, grandfather of Henry Beetle Hough. We used to go there for Sunday dinner sometimes. The only trouble was that she was a most particular woman; everything had to be just so. The table always looked very elegant indeed with its damask linen, polished silver, crystal ware, roast leg of lamb, and quince jelly, and all that, but it took her forever to get the food on the table. I was ravenously hungry and could hardly stand it.

In summer we went to Oak Bluffs by trolley. We would get on at the Seamen's Bethel and take it as far as the bridge. That cost a nickel. After the bridge, which we crossed by foot, we paid another nickel and took another trolley the rest of the way to Oak Bluffs. Those were the days when a nickel was a nickel. The older girls, the teen-agers, didn't mind the change of trolleys, since the conductors were handsome college boys. I even knew a girl who married one of them.

RUTH: An evening jaunt to "Cod City" — the old name for Oak Bluffs was Cottage City — was one of the summer's big events. Saving up fifty cents for it took practically all summer. For that reason it was usually late August before we could go. Occasionally Mother would go over on a Sunday to hear some famous preacher at the Tabernacle, and one of us girls would go along. Being Sunday, there wasn't much to see but people walking about in their Sunday best. Still, it was pleasant to see all the fancy dresses and hats. Also, the ride on the trolley was fun. However, it wasn't to be compared with our evening spree we had been looking forward to since winter.

Spending our fifty cents was a matter of fancy budgeting — a little like the twenty-five cents we invested in fireworks on the Fourth of July. Twenty of the fifty cents had to go for the trolley. The remaining thirty had to cover rides on the Flying Horses (with luck you'd catch the brass ring for an extra ride or two), a popcorn bar at Darling's, and a fifteen-cent dish of ice cream at Rausch's. The last was a dream of elegance come true, for when we were seated around the marble-topped table, in would come a handsome young man in a white coat to take our order. He would bring tall glasses of ice water for each of us and colorful paper napkins. When the tray of ice cream arrived, there would be a plate of sultana fruit cookies, which the waiter with a dignified flourish would place in the center of the table. Mr. Rausch presided over his establishment with Old World charm, and when he spoke to his daughter behind the bonbon counter, his broken accent made us girls feel gaga. We were careful to eat our ice cream with our little finger curled so that anyone who looked at us might be impressed.

With our money gone, except for the carfare home, the evening at Oak Bluffs was still only half over. There were still things to do and see that didn't cost money. We could traipse up and down Circuit Avenue and gaze at the tempting things in the shops. When it was time for the band to start playing, we'd hurry over to the park and saunter around arm in arm, or sit on the grass and just listen and watch the holiday crowd. Sometimes we were able to time our "Cod City" visit so that it came on Illumination Night, when the camp grounds and all the little houses around it were hung with hundreds upon hundreds of candlelit lanterns. The place was transformed into a world of enchantment, a fairyland, where almost anything and everything wonderful might happen any minute.

[Since Oak Bluffs is only three miles from Vineyard Haven, one may wonder why the daughters considered it such an event. to go there. More than physical distance separated the two places. Vineyard Haven was essentially a small provincial village. Oak Bluffs, on the other hand, was a spectacularly popular summer resort, brought into being and to a large extent sustained by the great religious revival meetings that encamped there in the latter part of the 1800's. Oak Bluffs had big hotels, restaurants, fine shops, and even a railway train to shuttle people to and from the broad sandy beaches on the south shore. When the religious fervor was at its peak, twenty thousand people were reported to have thronged the campground on Big Day, the final day of the summer's revivalist ceremonies. Times have greatly changed since then, and few landmarks remain to indicate the dimensions of Oak Bluff's former glory. Two big hotels were lost in fires. The train was discontinued during World War I, and the tracks were torn up and sold for scrap. One looks in vain for the shops that used to be there. And yet an aura of enchantment remains. Children still come to the Flying Horses and try to catch the brass ring. The old campground and the densely clustered gingerbread cottages surrounding it constitute one of the Island's most colorful showplaces. And on Illumination Night, when the cottages are strung with candlelit paper lanterns, it is plainly apparent to all but the most leaden spirited: magic is in the air. E.E.M.]

VIII

Christian Charity

GRATIA: For several days Ruth had been sick, confined to the small attic bedroom at the top of the kitchen stairs. It was a few weeks before Christmas, a Sunday, and it was snowing. We three girls were gathered in the kitchen, the warmest room of the house. Mother was upstairs tending Ruth.

Mother came down looking anxious. "Ruthie's no better," she reported. "Her fever is still up. I think it's time we had Dr. Butler take a look at her. Nina, run over to his house and leave word for him to come as soon as possible."

The Butler house was not far. Nina had only to cross William Street, skin through Captain Smith's, cross Spring Street, and there she was.

Dr. Butler came and went up to Ruthie with Mother. They were not up there long. When they came down Mother's face was white.

"What's the matter, Mamma?" I asked.

She couldn't get the words out.

"Your sister is very sick," Dr. Butler told us. "She has scarlet fever."

We were stunned. We knew what scarlet fever was. Our good friend Bennie Crowell had had it only recently. He had been delirious for several days. There was a long quarantine. Your hair could fall out. You could die. No disease was worse than scarlet fever.

Dr. Butler turned to Mother. "Mrs. Eldridge, the other girls must leave the house at once. We'll just have to hope they haven't been exposed already."

Mother looked at the three of us as if for the first time. "I'll send Nina and Mary around with a note right away to see who can take them in," she said.

"There's no time for that, Mrs. Eldridge," Dr. Butler broke in. "This is an emergency. There must be someone you can count on to help you at a time like this."

Mother thought a moment. "Aunt Lottie," she said. "Yes, Aunt Lottie, I think she'll do it and she has the room. All right, girls, get your clothes together as best you can. I have to write Aunt Lottie a note, and then I'll help Gratia."

We were ready in fifteen minutes. Naturally, we were very worried about Ruthie, but also we were rather excited. It was like an adventure. We bade good-bye to Mother and set out, each clutching her bundle of clothes, toothbrush, comb, and other necessaries.

Poor Aunt Lottie! Her mouth literally dropped open when she opened her back door and found us standing there. She was Uncle Henry Beetle's second wife and had never had children of her own. She took the note we gave her from our Mother, told us to wait, and went to consult

Uncle Henry. He was a retired whaling captain, a genial and delightful gentleman. He said of course we could stay.

When Mother wrote Father for suggestions of what to do, Father, from the safety of Boston, wrote back that now was the time for her good Methodist sisters to show their Christian charity.

Uncle Henry was as charming as ever, but Aunt Lottie's very particular housekeeping made us feel we had to ask before we even sat down or touched anything. We stayed with the Beetles a week, then we went to the Fosters down-the-Neck. Here the atmosphere was more easy-going and relaxed. Mrs. Foster had helped Mother when we were being born, and had taken care of us when we were very small.

Then came Christmas. What worse misery could there be than to be away from home at Christmas? I couldn't imagine any. Although we had little money, Mother somehow always managed to get the present each of us wanted. But it wasn't only that. It was the excitement of the preparation, the smell of pies, and especially fruit cake baking in the cookstove, and hanging up our stockings on Christmas Eve, and Father being there. I suddenly felt abandoned. Christmas Eve I cried myself to sleep. But when I woke in the morning, there was my stocking! Perched on top was a lovely new doll with her skirts carefully draped around the edge. Nina and Mary had dressed her for me.

After a week with the Fosters we were on our way again. The next Christians to be counted were the Smiths, Fannie and Alexander. Fannie was another of those very particular housekeepers, and a woman of uncompromising thrift to boot. It was said she saved more than Alexander earned. I recall our time there as one unrelieved hunger pang.

The sense of adventure had long since ended. We longed to be home again. Every afternoon we would go up to William Street, circle around in back of our house, and wait for Mother to come out and talk to us and tell us how Ruthie was. To see Mother and not be able to go up to her and touch her was almost more than we could bear. Ruthie was coming along fine. She waved to us cheerfully from the bedroom window. How we envied her! From time to time Mother gave us spending money. She would pour some silver in a cup, pour boiling water over it, then dump the contents out on the ground for us to pick up.

After the Smiths we were separated. I went to stay with Auntie Revel; Nina and Mary went to the Giffords. Betsy Gifford belonged to a special group in the church known as the "Holiness People." They aspired to perfection. Betsy was also poison neat, as we used to say. Auntie Revel was Betsy's opposite. She was a hearty, buxom, very outgoing person, and she loved children. In summer she made her dining room over into an ice cream parlor. Her ice cream was famous all over the island.

Mary and Nina had a short week at the Giffords. Early Saturday morning Betsy suddenly announced that this was the day she cleaned, and she couldn't have anybody around.

Mother foresaw the dwindling away of Christian charity and had written Father that he simply must come home and take charge. To his credit Father came at once. Upon reviewing the situation, he decided Auntie Revel was his best bet. At first she tried to object. After all, she had me, her mother, a lame husband, and two male boarders already. But Father could be very persuasive. The ones who were already doing twice their share were the ones you could get to take on extra, he always said. So the three of us stayed with Auntie Revel until the glorious day when the quarantine was lifted.

I remember the smell in our house as we walked in the door. To make sure there would be no lingering scarlet fever germs on our return, Mother had put sulphur on a shovelful of live coals from the cookstove and carried it around through all the rooms. It was a most unpleasant smell. But we didn't mind. We were home!

IX

The Barracks

GRATIA: Our home was a place where young people came a great deal. Father called it the barracks. Mother believed in children having a good time. There were often ten or a dozen children in the house. The back stairs went up from the kitchen, and that gave them a place to sit.

We played the usual games. There was post office, although we didn't play it much because it was an out-and-out kissing game. Then there was spin the cover — not a bottle, but a cover. There were two lines of people, and you had numbers, even for the boys, odd for the girls. You spun the cover and called your opposite number, that is, girls called boys' numbers and boys called girls'. If the person called failed to pick up the cover before it stopped spinning, then he or she had to pay a forfeit. When the spinning part was over, someone sat in a chair blindfolded while another held the forfeits up one by one. "A forfeit, a forfeit hangs

over your head; what shall the owner do to redeem it?"
Then the blindfolded one would say kiss a girl or do something foolish. That was spin the cover. We also played Up
Jenkins. Two sides sat opposite at a table. One person held
a coin concealed in his hand. The leader of the opposite side
would order certain hand motions for everyone on the
other team to make, such as "creepy crawly," "rainy
rainy," and "fencey fencey," designed to make the hand
that held the coin betray itself. Finally, the order would
come: "Slam bang down!" The whole team would bring
their hands down flat on the table, and the other side would
try to guess where the coin was. That was a very popular
game. When we finished with games, we would gather
around the piano and sing songs — "Paddy Duffy's
Lumber Cart," "Sweet and Low," "There is a Tavern in a
Town," "My Bonnie Lies Over the Ocean" — all those old
tunes.

Mother and Father were most definite about which people they considered good enough for us to associate with. It
was sometimes very sad. For instance, when we were
younger there was a little girl who lived across the street.
Her mother was nice, and she was a nice little girl. Her
father, however, came from a family of which Mother
didn't approve. The father's sister had been our nurse, and
she had a child by one of the sailors off the ships. Because
the little girl was near, I played with her a good deal, but
Mother said she was just trash. The Hillmans were another
family that lived close by. Lucy Hillman was Ruth's age and
was lots of fun. But Mother frowned on her because, she
said, her family was not as good as ours. Many of these
people had worked in the harness factory. They were poor
Irish, descendants of the 1847 potato famine, poorly edu-

cated, and therefore just not our class in Mother's view. Nearly all the families Mother and Father did approve of were Methodists! There were only one or two Baptists on the accepted list. In high school the Baptists were known as "the other crowd."

Other mothers with daughters had one idea, to get them married off. Mother was disgusted with such an attitude. She made no effort at all to get us married. I never had a serious beau. There was one boy I liked, a wild lad . . . . Actually none of the girls in my group had beaux. There were boys Ruth's age. There was really only one family in town with a boy my age that Mother considered socially acceptable. That was the John O. Norton family. They lived a few doors from us on William Street. Mr. Norton had been in business in Chicago and returned to the Vineyard on his retirement. He was a selectman at one time, and he was a great wit, Mother enjoyed him very much. If we asked her where she'd been when she was late coming home, she was likely to say, "Been talking to John O. Norton!" His son's name was Roy, but Roy and I were never special friends. After church it was the custom for the boys to line up outside. As the girls came along a boy would step up to his favorite and ask her if he could see her home. It was embarrassing to walk past that line of boys.

We had taffy pulls. We'd put the pan outside the back door to cool, and when we went for it, it wouldn't be there. I remember the whole thing would disappear, then later the pan would reappear empty. Somehow the boys were always able to smell when we were making candy. They, of course, were never invited. Taffy pulls were just for girls getting together.

I think we all had a happy childhood except perhaps

Nina. Being the oldest she bore the brunt of Father's anger. She wasn't happy when he was around, and was always afraid of him. As I said, Father was a man with a violent temper. He had many frustrations. People didn't seem to appreciate his navigational ideas. Mother had to humor him. As girls we were always taught to humor the husband.

X
Boarders

GRATIA: Mother was very independent. She was a leader in the village in public affairs. She was the first woman to speak in town meeting after women got the vote. Father admired her very much. He was quite willing for her to do what she wanted to in public things.

During the teen-age period, when Nina went away to boarding school, we had little money. Father's expenses in Boston were heavy getting his business started there, and we didn't have much to go on. So Mother decided to make the William Street house bigger. She borrowed money from the bank, had the house raised up a story and another floor built underneath. Our neighbors were worried about our being stuck up there on timbers. The very first night the house was raised we had a heavy storm, wind and rain to beat the band. In the morning we looked out the window and saw perhaps dozens of people looking up at us goggle-eyed. Nothing had happened. Mother wasn't worried. She was a very brave person.

When the work on the house was completed Mother announced: "We're going to take in boarders, summer boarders!"

It was a terrible thing for us. It hurt our pride dreadfully. But money had to be found for Nina's boarding school and for other things too.

We started taking in boarders the summer of 1895 and continued to do so for five years. I don't remember where the first ones came from. Ruth never got over it, she hated it so. She waited on table, and Mary and I did the chamber work. We hated it all. We hated especially having strangers there on our front porch. We couldn't have had more than ten at any one time, but ten was quite a crowd. Among ourselves we used to call them the "pesky boarders," or "p.b.s" for short. We had some very good times because we made friends with the people who came. Yet we hated them in our house.

XI
Limes And Loafing Places

GRATIA: One of the favorite hang-outs for the boys was the place that is now Mardell's Gift Shop. Tobacco, candy, and newspapers used to be sold there then. It was a kind of gauntlet for girls to run, for there were always comments.

Another favorite place was the steamboat landing. The boat left for the mainland at eight in the morning and returned at half-past four in the afternoon. It was the *Monahasset* when I was a girl. It was a side-wheeler. I never did understand the mystery of that thing going up and down at the top. I could not figure out what made the boat go. The young people loved to go down and watch the boat come in. It was considered great excitement. Mother would not allow us to go down to the landing. She thought girls who did so were not nice. Fortunately there was the drugstore, situated where the insurance office is, next to Leslie's. The drugstore had wooden venetian blinds through which we could peek and see who was coming off the boat. One of the girl clerks was a friend of ours and let us look as long as we liked. It was the best we could do under the circumstances.

[In summer today "the boat" comes in at least nine times a day, ten times on Fridays and Sundays. Yet it is still a source of fascination. You see young people getting a cone or a coke at the Harborlight and wandering over to the pier, just to see who comes off. If they are meeting friends, there may be a guitar and some banners or hastily painted sign: "Welcome, Bill and Jack!" "Hey there, Debbie and Ginger!" The measured approach of the vessel builds anticipation. Under no other circumstances is meeting friends more intense and exciting. By the same token, seeing friends off tends to be sombre and poignant. Such is the case in our household, anyway, and we have evolved a ritual to cope with it. We get up much earlier than usual and go to the Black Dog for a lingering final breakfast. A few minutes before departure time we walk over to the pier. We say our good-byes. Our friends board the boat and go up on deck. We shout messages back and forth. The whistle blows, and the boat begins to move. We wave, they wave. The boat gathers momentum and builds a wake. The figures on deck get smaller and smaller. As the boat rounds the breakwater we give one last wave. Then we turn away. E.E.M.]

Then there was waiting for the mail at the post office. Few people had lockboxes then, and we had to get our mail from the postmaster at the window. If the boat didn't run for a day or two, the mail accumulated, a crowd would assemble, and it became quite a social event.

On the corner opposite Cronig's was a grocery store. It belonged to Mr. Stephen Luce, father of the present Stephen Carey Luce. In the fall of the year Mr. Luce bought a hogshead of cucumber pickles. During school recess we'd tear down to the store to buy a pickle. They cost a penny each. We'd line up at the barrel, each of us with our penny in hand. There was a wooden dipper we'd roll round and round until the biggest pickle came to the top. Our children and grandchildren and their friends tend not to believe this. Especially that we got a big pickle for only a penny. Hence, we got to calling it pickle-barreling whenever someone told a tall story.

The first time I had a whole nickel of my very own I was so excited I couldn't decide what to do with it. I finally bought a chocolate bar, most of which melted in my hand before I was willing to eat it. After that, when I had a nickel I was more apt to spend it on pickled limes. I was passionately fond of them. Ships used to have them to protect sailors from getting scurvy, and I expect that's how they came to be sold in the town. The last place I remember that sold them was the shop where the boys liked to hang out. The storekeeper kept them in a small wooden barrel. The brine he got from the harbor. He simply dropped his bucket in and scooped it up. I remember once I got six limes for a nickel, but pretended to my chum I got only five. I gave her two and kept four for myself. But she was clever and knew what was going on. My conscience troubled me for a long time after that.

We also bought licorice — long, thin sticks of licorice. To us the zenith of gourmet delight was the combination of licorice and pickled limes!

I was nine when I had my first ice cream soda. My friend Hattie Weber treated me. Sodas cost ten cents. I enjoyed that soda so much and was so eager to get all of it that I bit a piece right out of the glass. I didn't hurt myself, but it was humiliating.

At that time the grocer sent his clerks out to each house in the morning to collect orders to be filled and delivered during the day. Milk was delivered for six cents a quart by a tall, handsome man who looked like a Viking. He lived in Lambert's Cove and came in all sorts of weather.

There were all kinds of stores on the Island, for it was something of an expedition to go off-island to shop. Village stores were important. Haines' Gift Shop, where Union Street comes into Main, was a big store in the old days. It was built by Captain Barnard Luce, a retired sea captain, and made into a dry goods store. There were no ready-made clothes, of course. In the middle of the store building there was a stairway to the second floor. On one side of the upstairs was the telephone. Father was a friend of the telegrapher, whose job at that time was most important. He offered to let me listen in, and I did. A man in Nantucket was talking to a fish dealer in Woods Hole. Terribly exciting! On the other side of the upstairs was the customs office. It was run by Captain Lorenzo Luce, a great uncle of Stephen Carey Luce, but no relation to Barnard Luce.

Stores were great loafing places. At Swift's grocery store, where Brickman's is now, there was a potbellied stove with chairs around it where people would gather. Where Shirley's Hardware is now there was a tobacco and newspaper shop run by a Matthew Chadwick, and he had a back room set up for loafers. These were old men who went in there, mostly retired sea captains. When Mr. Chadwick got too old to run the store and someone else took over, the men were so upset at losing their loafing place that they founded the Barnacle Club, which you see today above Ben Franklin's Five and Ten.

They used to grind grain at the feed store on Water Street. When the owner came out to wait on people, he would be all covered with flour. We used to call them the "floury people."

On the corner of Church Street and Main was where the Tashmoo Inn used to stand. It was set back with lawns at the front and side, and there was a vine-covered porch that ran around it. It was a pleasant place and very popular. However, just across the street was Renear's livery stable. The boarders complained of the smell to the innkeeper, and the innkeeper complained to the powers that be. But the innkeeper was not a popular man; he was a rather self-important sort and had no influence with the villagers at all. Walter Renear, on the other hand, grandfather of the present Walter Renear and Robert and Dixon, was very popular. I remember one of the lines in an old minstrel show: "Why is Walter Renear like a piano?" And the answer: "Because he's grand, he's square, he's upright!" The poor innkeeper had to move his inn half a mile to where it presently is on the West Chop Road. The name has now been changed to The Sandpiper. Mr. Renear continued with his livery stable until he went into the automobile business.

When I was a girl the population of Vineyard Haven was 1,200. Oak Bluffs was 1,000, and Edgartown was perhaps 1,300. West Tisbury was only about 500. Everything was drawn by horses. A trip to Gay Head by horse and wagon was an undertaking. Our doctor, Dr. Butler, attended pa-

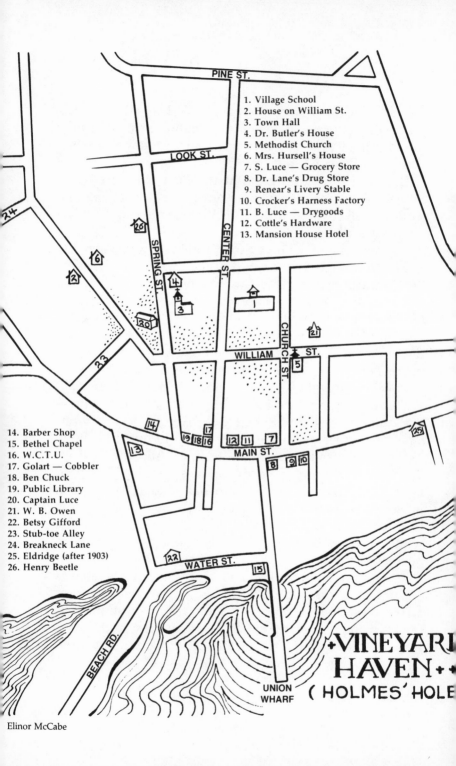

1. Village School
2. House on William St.
3. Town Hall
4. Dr. Butler's House
5. Methodist Church
6. Mrs. Hursell's House
7. S. Luce — Grocery Store
8. Dr. Lane's Drug Store
9. Renear's Livery Stable
10. Crocker's Harness Factory
11. B. Luce — Drygoods
12. Cottle's Hardware
13. Mansion House Hotel

14. Barber Shop
15. Bethel Chapel
16. W.C.T.U.
17. Golart — Cobbler
18. Ben Chuck
19. Public Library
20. Captain Luce
21. W. B. Owen
22. Betsy Gifford
23. Stub-toe Alley
24. Breakneck Lane
25. Eldridge (after 1903)
26. Henry Beetle

PINE ST.
LOOK ST.
CENTER ST.
SPRING ST.
CHURCH ST.
WILLIAM ST.
MAIN ST.
WATER ST.
BEACH RD.

+VINEYARD
HAVEN++
(HOLMES' HOLE

UNION
WHARF

Elinor McCabe

tients up there, nevertheless. He was truly a remarkable man. Mother admired him so much she named me partly after him. His first name was Winthrop, my middle name is Winthrop — Gratia Winthrop Eldridge. Ruth, who always had things figured out, said she never worried about being bad because Dr. Butler would never let her die.

Dr. Butler lived on the corner of Franklin and Spring Streets, next to the town hall. It was not his house originally. The house was built and lived in by the Howland family. John Howland had come to the Vineyard from the Cape as a carpenter during the whaling days. A young Vineyarder, Rebecca Luce, became enamored of him. One day when she was visiting her aunt who lived down by the shore, her aunt said: "What's this I hear about you, Becky, making eyes at John Howland! Don't you have anything to do with an off-Islander. You wait until spring when the boys come back from whalin'. Then you'll have your pick of some good ones!" But Becky paid no attention. She married John Howland. They had a son and three daughters, and one of the daughters married Dr. Butler.

Then there was Dr. Lane. Dr. Lane was the one who got mad at the telephone company and set up his own lines. He wore a top hat and a cutaway coat, and seeing him perched atop one of his poles making repairs he looked for all the world like a huge black crow. We always thought of him as a bit of a quack. His exchange was in the back of the drug store. He probably had forty subscribers, mostly his patients. He stayed active until about 1910.

And there was Dr. Leach. It was suspected that his practice was largely giving out whiskey to his patients. He lived on William Street, two doors down from the Pangburns.

Some years after he died the house went up for sale. We were looking for a place at the time and considered it. We went all through it. In the attic we came across Dr. Leach's old medicine bag. It had been there for years, and no one had noticed it. We found no whiskey, however.

XII
The Church

GRATIA: Our family had mixed feelings about church. Mother was a devout churchgoer, Father was a freethinker. But it was all right for Mother to do as she pleased in the matter. She had been brought up a Lutheran in the Middle West. Here there were only the Baptist and the Methodist churches. The Unitarian Church was not then functioning; the Episcopal Church had services only in the summertime. Mother didn't want to be immersed, so she joined the Methodists. She never enjoyed the denomination much, but that was what there was. We children went to Sunday School and church and young people's meeting. Nina and Ruth sang in the choir and Mary played the violin.

MARY: From the time I was a child my main interest was religion. I was seven when I began to question the doctrines of our church, and I had a hard time thinking and wondering. There were services at the church all day long on Sundays in the old days. There was a prayer meeting at nine in the morning, Sunday School at ten-thirty, a preaching service at two, young people's meeting at five-thirty, and then at seven-thirty an evening prayer meeting and a preaching service. I wanted to go to most of these. I remember my first time at the morning prayer meeting. I got as far as the vestry steps, and there I stood facing all the people, too bashful to go down and take a seat, and not one person thought to come and take me by the hand and help me. That rather frightened me and I decided not to go to morning prayer meeting after that.

GRATIA: They tried hard to save me, but I refused to be saved. You had to have a conviction of sin, then you got saved and lost the conviction. I couldn't understand the accumulation of sin. Since I said prayers every night to be forgiven my sins, how could there be any accumulation? Nina and Mary joined the church, but I said no. Mother didn't believe in infant baptism, so I've never been baptized. I was very unhappy at the endless meetings where they hammered away at heaven and hell. However, I continued to go to Sunday School until I was in my twenties because church was the social center. You saw all your friends there.

Then, of course, we had the Epworth League, which had sociables, and that was wonderful. And bean suppers. They were a great item in the winter social calendar! The church ladies put them on to raise money. Beans and brown bread and pickles and coffee and cake. Cost, twenty-five cents. However, if you brought a cake, you could bring another person, and each of you got in for only ten cents. It was known as "going on a cake." Also, there was a deduction for bringing a pot of beans — I forget how many could go on a pot of beans. I think they couldn't have made much money, but they were great social occasions. Usually we girls would have to scrape up the twenty-five cents each, for Mother wasn't much on cake baking. She was a good cook in other ways, but not in cakes and pies.

RUTH: On Wednesday nights throughout the year, regardless of weather conditions or family demands, off Mother would go to prayer meeting. It was like a vessel in uncertain weather breaking her anchorage and sailing off to some sheltered harbor for quiet and peace. Once in a while we girls would go along with her. The vestry was always warm, and when the minister read the Scripture and did the praying I would get very sleepy and lean over on Mother's shoulder. But when the little organ began to play a hymn, I was wide awake, for I loved to sing. I didn't know the words too well, but I could follow along with Mother's strong voice like a bobbing tender tied to a sturdy ship.

After the contribution plate was passed the meeting was in the hands of the congregation for testimonies. In our prayer meeting all the brothers and sisters were supposed to testify according to what was expected of church members, without deviation or variation from the theme of Christian living according to Methodist doctrine. Testimonies were as variable in content as the people who gave them. Some spoke with great humility of the saving grace of Jesus in their own lives. Some spoke of a special revelation of power through prayer to meet some personal crisis or tragedy. A few just repeated some Bible verse, affirming its truth by their own experience. Occasionally some brother who loved to take the floor and exhort would choose a Bible verse and proceed with a thumbnail sermon — something for personal consumption and benefit to his listeners.

People were wont to sit in the same seats year after year, and I often wondered what would happen if someone absentmindedly, or some stranger, sat down in a seat belonging to some Methodist old-timer.

There were two seats in the first row where a couple always sat. She was a tiny woman and he was a great big chap — a second husband, who, "they said," had been a bit wordly" in his past, but who on wedding the little woman had been speedily converted, a lost sheep brought into the fold. They never missed a Wednesday night, and he was the first on his feet to testify, his voice husky with embarrassment. It was a good thing he sat in a front seat and all you could see was his broad back, for his face was scarlet.

There were two elderly sisters, "saints" of the church, who were always there to take their seats early in the middle of the back row. They were of the meek-and-mild variety of old maids, so shy and shrinking it was no wonder they never married. I mean, they just shrank away if a man looked at them. I suppose that was the reason they sat where they did, so they would be protected on all sides when they got up to give their testimonies. Nobody ever heard what they said, and they had to hold on tight to the chairback in front of them in order to get through the testimony.

By contrast there was the man who for years was most prominent in church affairs. There he sat in the same seat he had occupied ever since as a young man he had "become a Christian." His testimony was given with an air of assurance, for he seemed to know he was on the Lord's side, or vice versa, safe and secure. Church members stood a bit in awe of this brother, for the Lord had showered him with material benefits, and he was the largest contributor to the church treasury. This fact was not to be sneezed at. Also, he had a stylish wife, who kept their fine home in perfect order, never letting it get messed up with church sociables or sewing circles. It was believed by the little children — Methodist, that is — that this gentleman was God and that he lived in the belfry.

In regular attendance at prayer meeting was an elderly bachelor with an impressive red mustache. He had enjoyed the distinction of living in Boston before retiring to the Vineyard, and he certainly didn't want the brothers and sisters to forget it. When he rose to his feet to testify, he would clear his throat in a leisurely fashion to give his listeners time to come to attention, and then in a pompous voice he would begin: "When I was in Boston and walking down Washington Street...." It would be a thought that had come to him, which, with a bit of maneuvering on his part, could be turned to good account as to his experience as a Christian. Sometimes it was Tremont Street he had been walking down, but always it was Boston.

Most members, however, elected to offer up a prayer instead of facing up to the people who might have doubts about their testimony. It was much simpler, too, for you didn't need to be too personal in prayer, and because your eyes were closed, you didn't see the reaction of your listeners. Also if you sat in an end seat you could kneel on the nice carpet in the aisle.

Oh, but when Sister Betsy Gifford raised up her voice in prayer, you just had to listen, and though I was supposed to close my eyes, I just had to peek too. I was fascinated by the way her hair was stretched back in a bun, so tightly that it seemed to pull all the wrinkles out of her face. It was her neck, however, that really held my attention, for as her voice got louder and louder, the veins in her neck swelled and swelled until I thought they would burst and I wanted to see when they did. When she shouted "Hallelujah!" would probably be that time. She would begin her prayer with serenity as she conversed with her Lord. Soon that serenity changed to ecstatic fervor as she named over the joys of her Christian life. The fervor softened to tender pity remembering the lost sheep, the unsaved souls, and compassionate tears streamed down her face as she exhorted the kind Shepherd to seek the lost sheep and bring them into the fold. Finally, in abject humility she bowed her head and repeated as she always did: "God, be merciful unto us and bless us and cause His face to shine upon us, Amen." And all the people said together, "Amen, Sister Betsy." Old Mrs. Allen would shout, "Oh, praise the Lord!"

The last time I went to Wednesday night prayer meeting with Mother was just before Easter when the minister was to leave for another parish, having served the church just one year. It was rather a sad occasion, for the church membership was divided as to the value of the minister's services. Mother felt one year was too short a time for a minister to prove his worth, but she was in a minority. All day before the meeting Mother called on members urging them to attend the meeting. Three of us girls went to help fill up seats and to show our friendship to the departing family. I was thirteen at the time.

There was a fairly good attendance at the meeting, but many of them were men and women of the opposition, and they took their seats with an air of virtuous determination. I wondered what their testimonies would be. I wondered if the spirit of the Savior could shine through those set faces.

The time for testimonies came, and Mother spoke first in her warm and loving manner about the minister's dedicated service to the congregation and how fortunate they were to have had him, and then one by one the few friends of the minister followed with their testimonies. Then there was a long pause. You could hear the big clock on the wall ticking away as the seconds and minutes passed and silence reigned. The poor minister stood there facing his flock with such a sad look. I could hardly bear the lump in my throat and my pounding heart.

The minister's wife, sitting next to Mother, began to sing in her low, rich voice:

Along the River of Time we glide . . . .

The minister with his fine tenor joined her, and then others joined in:

Along the River, along the River
The swiftly flowing resistless tide
The swiftly flowing — the swiftly flowing!
And soon, ah soon the end we'll see
And soon 'twill come, and we shall be
Floating — floating
Out on the Sea of Eternity.

My thoughts were turned for the first time to the "River of Time" and the "Sea of Eternity." I saw now we were on that River of Time! And what cruel undercurrents there were to that "swiftly flowing resistless tide," undercurrents of hardness of heart, of failure, and of grief! Why, there were all kinds of undercurrents to the River of Time, as at South Beach, where people drowned through ignorance of the undertow and lack of strength to combat its force. Everyone, I too, was being swept along that River of Time into the Sea of Eternity. Oh, the sound of that clock as it ticked off the seconds, seconds that could never be reclaimed or changed or lived over. And soon, too soon — the Sea of Eternity! I felt an upheaval in my stomach. With a shiver I reached for Mother's hand.

I never went to a mid-week prayer meeting after that one. I hadn't the courage.

XIII
Christmas

RUTH: The year I was fifteen an evangelist of unusual power (plus personal magnetism and handsome face) converted us teen-agers from slumbering Christians to zealous missionaries and crusaders. Seven of us banded together and formed a society we called the Loyal Workers, with the motto "Haud ye leal," "Hold yourselves true." For our crusading purpose we adopted the Biblical verse, "Let your light so shine before men that they may see your good works and glorify your Father which is in Heaven." We confided in our Sunday School teacher our ambition to save the world (particularly the young men of the village), and after a very serious talk he arranged for us to have an altar meeting that consecrated us and our crusade. We held our meetings on Sundays before evening service and older people of the church, especially our parents, came and dulled our spirits, so we had to include in our notices, "No one over the age of twenty-one allowed."

GRATIA: Members of the Epworth League came around and asked the Loyal Workers if they would combine, and the latter refused. Ruth got out of humor with the church and wouldn't have any more to do with it. She did sing in the choir, but she wasn't active in anything else. Of course the Loyal Workers was a religious society. Whenever Ruth did anything we didn't think was very good, we'd say to her with sarcasm, "You're a hefty Loyal Worker! You're a hefty Loyal Worker!"

RUTH: Our committees visited the sick with floating islands and pink gelatin. We also organized a supper. When the ham gave out and twenty-five hungry boys and girls got mad and demanded their quarters back, we decided to give up the whole idea of suppers. We circulated a petition, an agreement between males and females, the former to give up smoking, the latter to give up candy. We tried it for a month and then gave it up because there was evidence that both groups were breaking their contract. There were long, serious talks and letters exchanged with the young men, urging them to turn over a new leaf and not spend so much time on the tugboats at the wharf, where we suspected card playing, swearing and — maybe drinking!

GRATIA: We had a lovely time at Christmas. The Christmas Eve party at the Methodist Church was one of the loveliest things. It was one of the few times I was allowed to go out after dark. I can remember coming home and seeing the brightest star and thinking it was the Star of Bethlehem.

We looked forward to the Christmas Eve party all year. They always held it early in the evening, much to my disgust, because I thought for once they might let us stay up late. There were two enormous Christmas trees. Each mother brought presents for each of her children, and with so many children both trees were loaded with presents. There was a Santa Claus. The Sunday School superintendent would bring in bulletins: "Now we hear Santa is at Gay Head ... now he's passing Lambert's Cove ..." and so on. Finally, with a sudden deafening chorus of delighted screams from us children, he would burst in. That was toward the end, however. Before that there were speaking pieces, singing, and other forms of entertainment. Santa came, we had the presents, and then we had the ice cream. That was a treat! There was no place on the Island where you could buy ice cream in winter. It was either brought in from New Bedford, from a company called Bates, or some of the ladies made it. Then I remember going home afterwards and seeing the stars. I believe I was five at that time.

RUTH: When Christmas came we decided to celebrate by early morning caroling to the whole village. The idea was enthusiastically endorsed by all seven Loyal Workers, and the familiar carols were diligently practiced in preparation. When my friend Beth and I set out at four o'clock Christmas morning to rouse the others, however, each one had a sleepy excuse that could not be broken. Under the circumstances we decided to let our sisters join us. Beth had two and I had two who had been very envious of our daring romantic plan, and they got up in a hurry, tickled as could be. Since the sisters had not been in on the rehearsals, we agreed to sing only the first verses, which they all knew. Gratia knew all the words, to be sure, but she never remembered the tune that went with the words.

Beth and I had already been out a good while in the very cold morning air, and when the six of us finally started out, we were rather red of nose and cold of feet. But we were courageous and undaunted by the morning dark and cold, for Beth had reminded me, "Let our light so shine, Ruthie!" And out into the darkness we went, our sisters trailing happily behind. "Isn't it just too Christmassy," I overheard Beth's sister Emily say. "We can see the star in the East just like when it looked down on the baby Jesus, and when we start to sing, we're like the angels who sang, you know, 'Peace on Earth!' "

Our first stop was at the intersection of Spring and William Streets, where we knew there were shut-ins. There was an old man who was said to indulge in an annual Christmas drinking spree, the only one he was known to have. His wife died years before on Christmas morning, and in order to tide him over the anniversary he got very drunk and slept all day. Soon after we started to sing a light appeared upstairs in a nearby house, and then the cracked voice of old Mrs. Smith called out to us, "God bless you girls, Merry Christmas!"

On we went to a special place where there was an invalid we had often visited with our pink gelatin. No light appeared at her window, but her daughter later told us that at that very time her mother had had a wonderful dream that she had died and gone to heaven and that she had heard the angels singing.

After a few more stops with varying responses from the dark houses and the barking of dogs, who of course didn't know anything about Christmas, we thought we should visit the Marine Hospital, because we could see a light there. Tenderhearted Mary said, "Just think of those sick sailors away from home!" and we sped across the fields thinking how cheered the sick sailors would be to hear us singing. The northeast wind nearly blew us off our feet, and my front tooth began to ache like sixty, but we got in the lee of the hospital ell where the light was and started in with "Away in a Manger." The nurse opened the door a crack, and when we had finished she called, "Merry Christmas!" How happy we were as we returned to town for the last two stops.

We huddled together in Mrs. Betsy Gifford's backyard and opened up with "Oh, Come All Ye Faithful." Out came Mrs. Gifford and joined us. By now we were very cold and wanted to cut it short. To our dismay Mrs. Gifford dropped to her knees on the frozen ground and lifting her face to the heavens began to pray. She prayed fervently that we might forsake the sins of the world and follow in Jesus' footsteps. I'm afraid we weren't very responsive. We didn't feel at all sinful, and the only footsteps we were interested in following just then were the footsteps that led to the church belfry, our last stop, where we meant our voices to carry to all the vessels in the harbor — at least to the tugboats lined up at the wharf. Up to the belfry we climbed, and there, as the rays of the rising sun spread throughout the town, our hearts were warmed to the glory of the earth and all the people who dwelt therein. We sang out, "Joy to the world, the Lord is come, let earth receive her king!" When we had finished the verse, we heard from the tugboats a response that thrilled us through and through. All kinds of noises saluted us — foghorns, dinner bells, whistles, and crashing of pans like cymbals. It was a din that surely wakened all the town. But we didn't care! It was Christmas morning and the joy we had sung from the belfry was returning to us manyfold, and we started for home skipping and laughing and bubbling over with good feeling.

XIV
Menemsha

GRATIA: In 1900, when I was fifteen, Mary was invited by a group of other young women, mostly older than she, to go up to Menemsha and take a house and spend a week or ten days. That gave us the idea. So Mary, Ruth, and I, and three friends who were as adventurous as we, and two others, eight of us in all, took a house at Menemsha. How we loved it! We used to clean our faces and brush our teeth by a little brook and hang our towels on the trees. The little brook is still there, but it has changed a great deal. There were no summer people then. We were the object of a great deal of interest. The fishermen were very good to us. They invited us along when they went out to haul in their nets. I went only once because I got seasick. The hot sun and bobbing up and down were too much for me.

We used to walk over through the woods to the center — meaning the post office and general store combined. It was great fun to have to feel for the stepping stones with our sneakers. I remember our first visit to the general store when we saw several people sitting around not making a sound, only smiling, just smiling away. It was awhile before we realized they were deaf and dumb. At that time there were seventeen deaf-and-dumb people at Menemsha. They were born there and mostly related. Interestingly, the deafness and dumbness has died out. The same families are there, but none of the members is deaf and dumb. Once we were walking to the center by the road, which was longer, and a man picked us up. Both his mother and father had been deaf and dumb. He made noises to his horse, the strangest noises you ever heard.

We wore our bathing suits practically the whole time, and got very tan. Once when we were sitting beside the road, some people passed us, and we overheard one of them say, "Oh, look at those Indian girls!"

In those days they had neighborhood conventions run by the churches once a month during the fall, winter, and spring. That September there was to be a convention at a little church not far from where we were in Menemsha, and Mother sent a message by the telephone in the general store that she planned to attend, since she had not seen us for several weeks and missed us. A woman offered us a ride from the center to the church on the day of the convention. As we were riding along she remarked to us: "I wonder if your mother will like seeing you in bathing suits." Oh, yes, we said, Mother wouldn't mind. But when we arrived and Mother saw us, she was horrified! She took us around to the back of the church and kept us there the whole time we were there. The bathing suits came up to the neck, sleeves halfway to the elbow, skirts to the knees, and, of course,

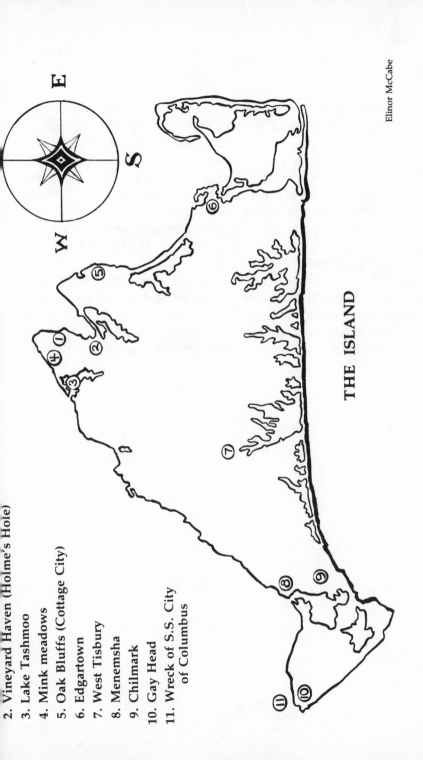

2. Vineyard Haven (Holme's Hole)

3. Lake Tashmoo

4. Mink meadows

5. Oak Bluffs (Cottage City)

6. Edgartown

7. West Tisbury

8. Menemsha

9. Chilmark

10. Gay Head

11. Wreck of S.S. City
    of Columbus

THE ISLAND

Elinor McCabe

stockings and sneakers. Even so, it was considered shocking for us to go to the convention in our bathing suits.

The next year we went to Menemsha again. As we were getting ready to go, we made friends with a young fisherman who said he would take us up in his boat. We were delighted. We got as far as West Chop, however, and the current was too strong for his one-lung engine. But that didn't bother us too much. We simply went ashore and played duck on the rock until the tide changed and the current went the other way.

We stayed in a tent the second year. There was a tremendous thunderstorm, and the tent would have been washed away had the fishermen not come and dug a drainage ditch around it for us. They brought us over hot oatmeal for breakfast every morning, the fishermen did.

XV
Visiting Dignitaries

GRATIA: There were a number of big events during the year, but the one that made the most stir was Memorial Day. We were only thirty years away from the Civil War, and Mother remembered it very well. It had made a deep impression on her, because she was then living in southern Ohio, and her family knew copperheads, those, that is, who sympathized with the South. On the Island, as all over the country, we had the Grand Army of the Republic, the organization of the veterans. We also had the sister organization, the Women's Relief Corps. On Memorial Day we sometimes had two observances. The towns took turns having the Big Day, the main celebration. When the Big Day was in one of the other towns, then Vineyard Haven would have an early service in the Baptist Church as well.

I remember one Memorial Day when the Big Day was in Vineyard Haven. The procession came right by our house because we were on the street that led to the cemetery. Mother was always very patriotic. She got the big flag that Father used to have in his store and with great difficulty draped it over the house in front. It took her a long time to get the position just right, and she secured it by putting the attic window down on it. Up the street came the procession. When it got nearly opposite our house, Ruth, in a burst of enthusiasm, ran up to the attic and opened the window. Down came the flag! Poor Mother! She had a hard time forgiving Ruthie for that.

When the procession had passed, we all followed along to the cemetery. There each veteran would take a group of us to a grave, and we would lay flowers on it. Finally, there would be the playing of taps for the unknown soldier.

After the Memorial Day service we went on a picnic. We used to go to Tashmoo at the head of the lake where the pumping station was. The engineer who took care of the pumping station — who must have been a rather lonely man — was always glad to have us come. The minute we got there he'd hang a swing from one of the tree branches. He took us in the pumping station and showed us the marvelous machinery. We saw very little of that sort of thing in those days. Downstairs there was a big tank, and in the bottom of it there was a steel pin that had never rusted.

Then there was the Fourth of July. It used to be that you had to get a permit from the selectman's office if you wanted to set off firecrackers. Mary and I loved to set off firecrackers. We were, in fact, the only girls who did. There were always derisive remarks from the selectmen as we lined up for our permits. We were the only girls in a line of small boys. But we didn't care. We had to fire off some firecrackers. It was a passion we inherited from Father.

Once he came home with a hundred packages of firecrackers. His rheumatism was bothering him rather a lot at the time. I remember him sitting out back under his umbrella—it was a very warm day — shooting them off one after the other. When he was finished we found the umbrella riddled with little burn holes.

I especially remember one Fourth of July observance. It was held in the open field by Causeway Road where we went coasting in winter. The speaker stood at the top of the hill and addressed the people gathered below. What made this particular observance notable was the speaker — or rather how he came to the Vineyard.

His father was a fisherman who lived on Hatch Road. He and his wife had always wanted children, but not succeeded in having any. One day Mrs. Morse, the fisherman's wife, heard that a neighbor was going to Boston, and she went to him and said, "While you're there, I wonder if you'd be willing to get something for me."

"Of course," he said. "What do you want me to get you?"

"I want you to bring me a baby," she said.

"A what? A baby?"

"Yes," she said. "I want you to go to one of those foundling homes and get me a baby."

The man said all right, he would. He got a baby, and with the help of a sugar teat brought it back to the Vineyard. The baby grew up to be a handsome young man. One day he came into Father's store and said, "I want to study law and become a lawyer." That was an extraordinary thing for a simple fisherman's son. But the fisherman mortgaged his house and sent his son to school, and Will Morse became a successful lawyer and eventually a state senator. He was our Fourth of July speaker that day.

RUTH: Mrs. May Alden Ward, the illustrious lecturer on current events, had been engaged by the Want-to-Know Club (of which Mother was then president) to give her lecture in the town hall. We were to entertain her. Mother always offered hospitality to important off-island people like lecturers and presiding elders for the dual purpose of exposing her island-bound daughters to persons of culture and brains and for a bit of intellectual stimulus for herself. The whole week previous she had worked to get the house in apple pie order, keeping us girls busy washing windows and polishing silver and doing whatever she could think of to make our house as attractive as possible.

The day came for Mrs. Ward to arrive. By the time the boat whistled that afternoon at four-thirty the dining table was set with the best linen and china and we girls were done up in our Sunday best. Father was delegated to meet Mrs. Ward at the boat with one of Mr. Renear's fanciest carriages. When they drove up to the gate we were all on the porch to meet her. She was a fine-looking woman, very stylish, and as Father helped her alight from the carriage, her elegant manner and cultivated voice made me feel terribly country bumpkinish. After the introductions, Nina, in accordance with advance instructions, carried Mrs. Ward's bag into the guest room while Mary and I went to fetch the tea tray. Tea was for two only. It was Mother's cherished time for socializing, and for the guest it was a bit of refreshment.

After tea Mrs. Ward retired to her room to rest, and Mother came into the kitchen to oversee the final preparations for dinner. She was a bit steamed up for her. You wouldn't call her frantic, because Mother was never frantic, but she was about as close as she ever got to that state. As

Nina   Mary   Ruth   Gratia

THE ELDRIDGE SISTERS

Courtesy of I. Saunders

Grandfather "Chart George" (l.) as a young man and
the "Captain" (r.) in his thirties

Sydna Saurbaugh Eldridge as Mother and as bride.

Nina (at 26) shocks
by riding astride

Mary at about 18

Ruth (at 15) — the
Loyal Worker

The youngest of
the four, Gratia, at
15

The first Eldridge house on Grove Street "down-the-Neck"

The family in 1898
Standing (l. to r.): Nina, Ruth, Mary
Seated (l. to r.): Sydna, Gratia, George

The William Street house with the "pesky boarders" on the veranda, the daughters (with friends) on the porch above, the Captain surveying it all from the picket fence

Gay Head Indians

The little train of the Martha's Vineyard Railroad.

After the Great Storm of 1898.
Top: The schooner *Newburg* with her bows jammed
through Union Wharf
Bottom: Wreck-strewn Vineyard Harbor

Bathing Beach and Sea View House at Cottage City
(now Oak Bluffs)

she hustled the raised biscuits into the oven and opened jars of piccalilli and quince preserve, she reminded us once again what our deportment was to be at supper. Then she darted into the back room to see if her mold of pressed chicken had become stiff, which it had. She deftly transferred the contents of the mold onto our best platter and bore it into the dining room and placed it in the very center of the table. Nina put the floating islands and frosted cake on the sideboard, and Mary took in the first batch of piping hot biscuits just out of the oven. Gratia and I did nothing but get in the way, and sure enough, Mary bumped into us and the biscuits went skittering all over the floor. We had them picked up in a trice, though, and Mother was none the wiser. Finally everything was in readiness, and for a few moments we quietly stood and marveled at our handiwork. Mother's face was aglow with pride.

As they say, "Pride goeth before a fall." After hanging from the ceiling for thousands of meals, the lamp over the dining room table suddenly chose this moment to slip its mooring. Down it came with a bang and a crash and a tinkling of glass, smack in the middle of Mother's pressed chicken. For a brief moment we were in darkness. Father came bursting in, followed presently by Mrs. Ward, and the light from the parlor was quite enough to see what devastation had been wrought. Broken glass and soot were on everything, and kerosene was oozing in all directions. But the greatest devastation was to Mother's face. I have never seen such pain and distress.

Mrs. Ward went immediately to her and put her arms around her. "My dear Mrs. Eldridge, I can't tell you how sorry I am. Believe me, I can see what an absolutely beautiful dinner it was!"

"Nina, Mary," said Father peremptorily, "bring the lamps from the parlor. Ruth, Gratia, gather the silver and unbroken china and take them into the kitchen." We leapt to do as he said. "Now, Sydna, you and Mrs. Ward each grab a corner of the cloth at that end, Nina and I'll manage this end, and we'll just move this whole mess into the back room and forget it until tomorrow."

Mother was horrified. "Not through the kitchen, George!"

"Of course through the kitchen, that's the only way there," Father retorted. Mrs. Ward, like the good sport she was, had already positioned herself at her corner.

"By the way," Father said as they started toward the kitchen, "how about that can of tongue you've been saving? With that, the biscuits I smell in the oven and some of your good, hot coffee, I believe our distinguished guest can weather the evening in fine shape."

GRATIA: I was just thirteen when the Spanish-American War came along. There was not too much excitement over it. Only one boy from the Vineyard went. There was a small telephone office next to where the post office now is. They would get the news over the telephone and write it on a little blackboard in the window. The news was full of the taking of ships. I didn't realize they were just merchant ships. But it allayed any fears we had. We took a ship practically every day. There were two girls in town who had cowboy hats like the Roughriders, with crossed guns in front, and I remember feeling very envious of them. The only other thing I remember about the Spanish-American War was Admiral Dewey's entering Manila Bay and all the fuss there was afterwards, the raising of money for a house for him, his marrying a Catholic, and dying and leaving the house to her, and the people not liking it.

XVI
Rich and Poor

GRATIA: We had our share of eccentrics. There was Ben Charlie, who might be seen most any day tip-tupping along the streets of our neighborhood in a very ladylike manner, perhaps wheeling a baby carriage. I remember one bawdy acquaintance of his calling across the street, "Hey Charlie, you a wet nurse?" Poor Charlie giggled and blushed. Harassed housewives had Charlie come in and do the dishes and tidy up the kitchen, at which he was said to be very efficient. He was pretty good with a crochet hook too. But the thing we remember Charlie for best was his christening of the two little lanes that run from South William Street to Main Street. One, which was mostly sand and stones, he christened Stub-toe Alley. The other, which was equally hazardous to navigate, he christened Breakneck Lane. Stub-toe Alley has since been paved and is called Camp Street. We older folk still call it Stub-toe Alley. Breakneck

Lane, though unpaved, is a pleasant dirt road, but it has never been renamed.

Then there was Ben Chuck. His real name was Ben Dexter. He was a short, thick-set man with bowed shoulders who had once been a whaler. In his youth he had scarlet fever, and it affected his speech so that only those who knew him well could understand him. Ben Chuck owned the piece of property that extends from the corner of Centre and Main to Yates' Drug Store and is now occupied by the Chowder Bar and the Bunch of Grapes Bookstore. The corner building has essentially the same shape it had in the eighties and nineties. The rest of the building was different. It used to be a long, low, shingled affair. It consisted mainly of a single long room. At one end of a shelf was a large beautiful model of a white steamship. At the other end was a model of a full-rigged ship. Ben Chuck rented this room out to the WCTU (the Women's Christian Temperance Union) ladies. The WCTU was a flourishing organization at that time. They used it for their meetings and also for a reading room and a game room for the young men of the town. Behind the building was a lean-to; this was where Ben Chuck lived. They said he carved out a hole for himself and crawled into it at night. But Ben Chuck was a genius with a penknife. The steamer and the full-rigged ship were evidences of his talent. What interested us most, and was there in plain sight for all to see, was Ben Chuck's garden. And a most unusual garden it was. At the back of the building — now used for a parking lot — Ben Chuck had made five mounds, grassy mounds, which were flat on top. On each mound was a wooden statue he had carved with his penknife. I remember only that one was an Indian and another was a lady. They were beautifully carved and painted.

There weren't many what you'd call poor people in Vineyard Haven. Anyone who didn't have enough money to support himself was "on the town," as we called it. We had a poor house up on the Edgartown Road, but I never knew anyone who went there. There were people in straitened circumstances. There was a woman who lived opposite us, for instance. Her husband had left her without money and with a young daughter to raise.   One thing she did to earn money was to crochet the fringe on pink shawls. I remember seeing her with her lap full of pink yarn, crocheting away on those things. Another thing she did was to attach a bit of string to marking tags. I don't recall how many she had to do for ten cents, but I do remember it was a great many. Another woman, an older woman, used to put up hulled corn and bring it around to sell it by the pint. It was a large kernel variety of corn, mixed with saltpeter, I believe, and was very good. Both these women had a really hard time.

At the other end of the scale were people who lived in far from straitened circumstances. There was the Owen family. They built the big house that used to be where Havenside is. They had a son, Will Owen. Will went into business in New York and somehow managed to get the European agency for the Victor Talking Machine. He took his whole family abroad, and they lived five years in England. They always sent their laundry back to the Vineyard to be done, though. Some say it was Will's dog you see in the advertisements listening with cocked ear to "His Master's Voice." True or not, Will made a lot of money in a short time. Of course, the thing was a mint. Everybody wanted a talking machine. They say he made three million. He came home with a white automobile, a chauffeur, two horses and a coachman, a gardener, an undergardener, and a butler whose name was Ruffles. He meant to set up as an English gentleman. They lived in his wife's house and built onto it. The Owens were like royalty. One thing Will Owen did was to buy controlling interest in the Martha's Vineyard Bank and have it moved to Vineyard Haven. Edgartown never forgave us for that. He established a factory below the bank and manufactured some sort of fancy leather. He imported a couple of Englishmen, one to be the manager, the other to be the bookkeeper. Some of the local girls were employed there. He also got into the hen business. They say he paid $1,500 for a cock. They bred prize hens and exhibited them all over the country. The first thing he built was Fourway, this building where I now live. It was built originally as a stable, but it wasn't used very long as such because soon horses went out and cars came in. What is now my apartment was first the hayloft, then it was converted into an office for the hen business. Will began to build hen houses around Tashmoo, and he built and built. He bought the land where Owen Park now is with the intention of building a great mansion there. There were three houses on that land, a cottage near the street and two big houses near the shore. Main Street was tied up all winter while those homes were being moved. Then he began to have not so much money. It leaked away, and he died of cancer in his fifties.

Will Owen had two sons, Paul and Knight. Paul was a very serious person, Knight was handsome and fun-loving. They both graduated from M.I.T.

Paul, while he was still in college, secretly married a beautiful girl who spent summers with her family in Oak Bluffs in the house now belonging to Senator Edward Brooke. Later they were divorced, and he married someone else. He worked in a bank in New York most of his life and died only a few years ago.

Knight, the younger brother, served in the Navy, married, divorced, and finally came back to the Island and lived with his mother. It was sad, for he was a charming boy.

One winter an attractive divorced woman with four children came to Vineyard Haven and rented a house belonging to Knight's aunt. Knight got to know them, and he and the divorced woman became good friends. She was a kindly, warmhearted person. She had been a summer resident and owned a cottage at Herring Creek.

Now in the old days there used to be great herring runs at the creek before the channel was dredged and enlarged. There were a number of huts down there. In the spring during the run men and boys used to go down, and everyone there got a share of the herring, just as they still do at Gay Head and Edgartown. They called it their "night in boots." Of course all that disappeared when they dredged the channel.

Before that, however, there was a man who lived down there in one of the huts. He was a bit of a hermit and considered rather odd, a character. We went to school together, so I knew him rather well. A strange boy. Anyway, this same divorced woman befriended him. She felt sorry for him, and he was very good with the children. The children were devoted to him. They loved to visit his shack and go rowing with him on the lake. He did all sorts of nice things for them.

The following summer when the woman returned to her cottage at Herring Creek, Knight Owen would go down and see her. There was no romance; they were just good friends. He liked the children; it was a pleasant place to go. But the hermit was very jealous of Knight. He was also fond of the woman, and he resented Knight's coming down there. One day Knight had just arrived and parked his car when the hermit came up behind him and shot him dead.

He was tried and convicted. He was sent to Bridgewater and was there for many years. Eventually they were going to let him out, but he didn't want to leave, and died there.

XVII
Politics

GRATIA: Father felt the future of the Vineyard lay in summer business. He would go into town meeting and beg them to make better roads. At that time the roads leading up-island were almost hub deep in sand. Rudolph Crocker, who was the owner of the harness factory and more or less the town boss because he employed so many people, persuaded the town to put scraps of leather from his harness factory on the roads to harden them. They did nothing of the sort, but he got rid of his leather scraps that way. At last the state decided to make a better road. In the summer of 1892 there arrived on the Vineyard a steamroller operation. It was the most exciting thing! I can remember it rumbling along up West Tisbury Road with a great following of children and older people behind. And it did make a good road. Incidentally, Father persuaded the town to make one good road to West Chop. They made it out of oyster shells.

It was a very pretty white road. In moonlight it was a most attractive thing, that white road leading to West Chop. But when Father begged them to make other good roads because they were going to have to depend on the summer population, they said: "You're crazy, Captain Eldridge. Whaling's going to come back! Whaling's going to come back. We're never going to have to depend on the summer population."

[Captain Eldridge put his money where his heart was. In 1898 he wrote and financed the publication of a booklet entitled *Martha's Vineyard: Its History and Advantages as a Health Resort.* It was a shoestring venture. We get an indication of this from the identity of the man on its front cover. It is not Captain Eldridge or some important Vineyard personage, as one might assume. It is B.A. Atkinson, a Boston furniture store owner, whose advertisement appears on the back cover. The extra money paid Captain Eldridge for the privilege of having the picture on the front cover in all probability represented the difference between the booklet's being printed and not being printed.

Today the Island population is 8,000 in winter, 48,000 in summer, and the summer people pay 60 per cent of the property taxes. E.E.M.]

The governmental structure of the town was the same in the 1890's as it is today. Quite often the selectmen were whaling captains who had retired from the sea, and they were very able men. Captain Gilbert Smith, who lived where the Bowditches live now, was a dean of selectmen. He was a selectman for many years. He owned what is now the town hall, Association Hall. Up until 1891 the town consisted of Tisbury and West Tisbury. It was all the Town of Tisbury. It was not a good arrangement, because West

Tisbury was full of farmers, Tisbury was full of fishermen, and they wouldn't agree. Town meeting was very important in those days. They met only once a year and alternated, one year at Tisbury, the next at West Tisbury. If it happened to be rainy weather when it was in West Tisbury, the Tisbury people wouldn't get up there and the West Tisbury people would vote things all their own way. The reverse would happen if it was rainy when the meeting was in Tisbury; the fishermen would have it their way. Although I was only five, I well remember how much talking there was about dividing the town. Finally, after the annual meeting of 1891, Father came home and said, "The town's divided!" Well, I didn't quite realize what that meant. I went downtown the next day fully expecting to see a barrier across Main Street "dividing the town." It has always seemed curious to me that West Tisbury is greater in area than Tisbury. With the exception of Gay Head, I believe Tisbury has the least area of any of the towns, and yet it has the biggest population. Which is unfortunate. Father was never a selectman. His business was in Boston, but he came home for town meeting and raised his voice. The townspeople always thought he was a little crazy.

Party affiliations never figured in town government. The Island was represented by a Republican representative always—nearly always, at least. I believe Gerry Studds to be the first Democratic congressman in the town's history. When I was young, to be a Democrat wasn't considered respectable. A few Democrats had come here with the harness factory. There were two others, Doctor Butler, a wonderful person, and the postmaster, also a very fine man. I remember saying to Mother once, "Why is it that Dr. Butler and Mr. Robinson are Democrats? They're such nice

people!" Mother said, "Well, they're war Democrats."
What that meant I do not know, but apparently it exonerated them from the taint that ordinarily attached to the breed.

We were dyed-in-the-wool Republicans. Mother was the first woman delegate to the Republican convention in Boston. Father stumped the state for Roosevelt when he ran in the Bull Moose Party. What he would have thought if William Jennings Bryan had been elected I hate to think.

The first national election I can remember was 1892. Cleveland against Harrison. I remember it very well because the boys had election caps, little visored caps, one for the Republicans and one for the Democrats. There was only one Democrat boy in school, and we used to yell at him, "Shoot the rat, shoot the cat, shoot the bloody Democrat!" And what was my horror and surprise when Cleveland was elected! A Democrat elected, I couldn't believe it! Father said that when the Democrats were elected the businessmen, the big businessmen, went to Europe on a holiday. There was very strong feeling against the Democrats. Today I consider myself a Democrat.

XVIII
Storm

GRATIA: The Bethel Seamen's Chapel has meant a great deal to my family throughout its existence.

The caretaker on Naushon Island had a store at Tarpaulin Cove to serve the ships that came to anchor there. Father used to go over there now and then to supply the store with charts and the *Tidebook*. On one of his trips he met, and got to know, a man from Woods Hole who used to bring over uplifting literature for the sailors to read. The man's name was Madison Edwards. Father suggested to him there was a much larger readership for his material at Vineyard Haven than at Tarpaulin Cove. Mr. Edwards said he had been thinking about that. Now, what Mr. Edwards's business was that he could afford the time to take that literature around I do not know, but he was a wonderful man. He got in touch with the Boston Seamen's Friends Society, and they decided to build a Bethel here in Vineyard Haven. I remember when it was being built. Mr. Edwards's family continued to live in Woods Hole, but he was here and stayed in a room in our house whenever he wanted to. He would come and talk to Mother about his problems of getting the Bethel built. It was 1895, 1896, along in there. Finally it was built. Not too long after that Mrs. Harriet Norris Goldberg gave a lot of money to make it a much nicer place.

Mr. Edwards had a boat with an engine in it, the *Helen Mae.* He would go out in all kinds of weather, taking his literature to the ships and bringing sailors in for the evening service. His wife was constantly worried. It was dangerous getting alongside the schooners in the dark. Now and then there would be a party in the reading room, and Mr. Edwards would come to Mother and ask her what she could do in the way of providing entertainment. Mary and Ruth played the violin, and they got their friends to go down and sing. I spoke pieces. I used to do some James Whitcomb Riley, and had a couple of dialect poems. Then we would pass around ice cream and cake. Mr. Edwards had two daughters, one Ruth's age, the other mine, and we became very good friends.

Mr. Edwards formed what he called the "'Hold Fast Society." Members wore a little button. It didn't mean you were converted, just that you were trying to live a better life. Sailors would meet each other all over the world and see that button.

The Boston Seamen's Friends Society is a Congregational organization, but they had all kinds of books and magazines for the sailors to read. Different societies in the village used to make "comfort bags" for the sailors. These were bags made of denim or chintz, and they had in them needles and pins, a thimble, a pair of scissors, darning cotton, and whatever else a sailor might need. They were given out at Christmas, and at other times too. It was no chore getting sailors to come ashore. They were bored to death staying on shipboard.

Then came the great storm of 1898. It struck on a Sunday morning, a blizzard early in the year, November 27. We girls always loved to go out in storms. (We were true daughters of father in this respect. Mother, being from the Middle West, could never understand it. She was a mother hen who'd hatched ducklings.) We told her maybe there was Sunday School. She said she was sure there wouldn't be Sunday School in such weather. But we kept after her. We said we had to see for ourselves. Finally, very reluctantly, she let us go. We went to the church to make everything legal and aboveboard, and then we made a beeline for the beach. It was snowing a wet snow, and the wind was blowing, but not so terribly hard, it seemed, as we made our way down there. When we reached the beach, however, suddenly we realized. The wind was from the northeast, and the harbor was wide open to the northeast. It was taking the full force of the storm straight on. Ships were ashore everywhere. Not far from the present ticket office lay a two-masted schooner called the *Mary Eldridge* — Mary's name. A big ship had crashed completely through the wharf and had its bow sticking out the other side. We couldn't believe it. Then, just as we were standing there, the strangest thing happened. The snow stopped, the wind abated, the sun came out! It stayed that way for about five minutes. But, during those five minutes we could see out into the harbor and realize what devastation had occurred there, too. More ships had capsized, masts were toppled, and a great sea was running — it was the most terrific sight!

When some of the townsmen who were sailors saw this, they decided they had to go out and try to get the men still aboard to shore. They patched up an old whaling dory and went out and brought men back from the ships. Later, toward nightfall, they decided they must make one more trip. When the dory was loaded, there were so many in it they feared they wouldn't be able to make it back to shore. One of the villagers, Frank Golart, David Golart's father, said, "I will stay." But the others all said, "No, we'll take our chances with everybody." They all came safely to shore. Frank Golart later received a medal.

There were shipwrecked sailors all over town. A lot were taken to the blacksmith shop so that the heat from the forge might warm them and get the circulation in their frozen limbs going again. Many were brought to the Bethel. They slept all over the floor. The townspeople rallied around and helped feed and entertain them. I tell you it's something to look at a roomful of shipwrecked sailors, perhaps as many as a hundred!

It was a terrific time. Next morning it was over. It was then they decided the harbor needed some protection from northeast storms and that they would build a breakwater. Father went to the State House and showed them where he thought the breakwater should go, off Huzzelton's Head, the high land. But the state people came down and put it where it is now. When Father came home and saw where they put it, he said, "They've ruined the harbor!" And of course they had. It's nothing compared to what it was. It's

hard to believe it was once the best harbor of refuge between New York and Boston.

Well, the work of the Bethel continued. Mr. Edwards
died, and his assistant took over. But after the building of
the Cape Cod Canal the ship traffic slackened a great deal.
In comparison with what it used to be, only a few ships
stopped. So the importance of the Bethel necessarily declined.

XIX
Love Story

RUTH: I must tell about Mr. Swift, my Sunday School teacher. I hesitate to do this, for from an adult point of view there is so much that is intangible, yet it was so real and vital to my growing-up days that I must make the attempt.

Mr. Swift was a grocer, and I loved to go on errands to his store. You might say it was because his store was filled with such good things to eat. There was a golden bunch of bananas, baskets of apples, a great pickle barrel, and, best of all, a showcase of candies, especially tempting to a five-year-old. But when Mr. Swift came to me with a smile and said, "And now, young lady, what can I do for you?" I grew inches taller, for no one else ever called me "young lady." After I had purchased everything on Mother's list, he would go behind the candy counter and say, "And what color gumdrop today?" "Pink, if you please, Mr. Swift," I would answer, and with my mouth full of lovely gum-drops, I would leave the store in a state of bliss.

I remember one day Mother needed a pint of vinegar to finish her piccalilli. She gave me a bottle and five cents and told me to run down to Mr. Swift's for it. "Now, Ruthie," she said, "I know you won't want to ask Mr. Swift for *wi*negar (I had a hard time with my v's), so I want you to practice all the way to the store and see if you can't say *vi*negar. If you can say it properly when you get home, I'll have a surprise for you."

I practiced all the way to the store, but I just couldn't do it right, and sadly I told Mr. Swift I couldn't. He sat right down on a cracker barrel and showed me how I had to grab my lower lip with my upper teeth, only I couldn't see very well because his mustache kept getting in the way. When I told him this, he laughed and laughed. Finally I got it, and I was so proud of myself I ran all the way home, burst into the kitchen, and said to Mother, "Give me the 'sprise, I can say it — vininer!"

"But Ruthie, where is the bottle?" Mother asked.

I had forgotten all about the bottle! I had to go back to the store after it, but I didn't mind a bit.

Sundays I would see Mr. Swift during opening exercises. He looked so nice sitting there in his best with his class of young ladies. After opening exercises he would take his class off somewhere for their lesson. How I longed to be old enough to be in that class! I felt I just had to do something to claim Mr. Swift's attention.

One Sunday when I was wearing a new summer dress — new to me, that is, for it was a hand-me-down from Cousin Nellie — I let my sisters go home without me. I slipped away and hid behind the big furnace at the rear of the vestry. I knew Mr. Swift was generally one of the last to leave. When nearly everyone was gone, I emerged from my hiding place and went and sat on the settee in the vestibule and waited.

I heard him coming down the stairs, and my heart began to go fast. When he saw me, he was very surprised. "Why, Ruthie," he said, "What are you doing here?"

"It's my rheumatism," I said with a quiver in my voice.

"Your what?"

"Well, you know," I said, "Father has awful rheumatism, and I guess it's like the Eben Norton children having red hair like their father. Sometimes I can't even walk at all. I don't see how I can get home very well. I can hop on my good leg, and there's fences I can lean against, but there's two roads to cross, and I was wondering what would happen if I fell down and couldn't get up!"

"Well," he said, all sympathy, "I guess I'll have to help you home. You can hop for awhile, and then maybe I could carry you for a bit — although you're getting to be a pretty big girl now."

"Yes," I said. And off we went, he holding my arm and I limping along, happy as a clam at high water, but knowing better than to show it.

When we reached home and Mother saw me leaning heavily on Mr. Swift's arm, she exclaimed, "Why, Mr. Swift, what has happened to Ruthie?"

"A little attack of the rheumatism, I think," Mr. Swift dutifully replied.

Mother gave me a funny look, but she had an understanding heart, and she said, "I see. Well, it was most good of you to help her. Now, Ruthie, if you feel able, you'd better hop into the dining room, as we've been waiting dinner for you some time."

Eventually I was graduated into Mr. Swift's class. How

proud I felt as he led us from the vestry to the auditorium for our lesson. We arranged ourselves in the two back pews in the southwest corner. Mr. Swift greeted us in a light and airy fashion, and with a sense of humor. Sometimes the humor was so subtle we didn't know just what he meant. It provided us girls with a subject for speculation on our walks home afterwards. Certainly Sunday School with Mr. Swift was a high point of our week. We were never ready to disband when the bell rang for closing time. I recall once, as we walked down the stairs together, his saying, "Now, that last question of yours, Beth, I'll have to think about it through the week and bring you an answer next Sunday. Perhaps there isn't any answer."

Mr. Swift was also leader of our class Friday evenings. We would meet in one another's houses and take turns reading the Scriptures and saying a prayer as we knelt beside our chairs. It was something of a trying time for me because my sister was in the class and she knew how selfish I was at times, and that made me self-conscious. At these meetings Mr. Swift would give a short sermon he had prepared, based on a Bible verse, and afterwards there would be questions and sometimes a very lively discussion. Sometimes some deep and troubling doubts were expressed. Then, with sympathy and understanding, Mr. Swift would renew our faith and our confidence that Christianity was the ideal of the human race, something to hold fast to.

The lesson period on Sundays was more formal. Leaflets issued by the Methodists each month would cover the reading matter for four Sundays, which we were supposed to study in advance.

Once I hadn't even looked at the leaflet and learned only as the lesson began that our reading from the Bible was about the naming of the baby Jesus at the time of circumcision. Mr. Swift asked me to read, and when I came to the word "circumcision," I said, "And what in the world is circumcision?" When Mr. Swift hesitated, I said, eager to show off my knowledge of Latin, "Oh I see, 'circum' means around and '-cision' means cutting. But it doesn't make sense. Cutting around what?"

Mr. Swift said quickly, "Oh, there are many ancient Jewish laws and customs we don't understand. Next verse, Jessie."

About two years later Mr. Swift was elected our representative at Boston. When he came home Sundays and appeared at church in his frock coat and striped trousers, I felt a barrier of formality had been thrown up between us that I was powerless to penetrate.

Once I overheard Mr. Swift say that he always listened for the lower voices,the altos, in the choir. His wife helped out with the Christmas and Easter music. She had a contralto voice of beautiful quality. I decided that I would switch from soprano to singing alto in the choir. But I found I couldn't carry the part, and I became discouraged. I had other discouragements, and as my counselor seemed too involved with other things to give me the attention I wanted, I became a backslider in the church.

I grew up, married, made a home in the Boston area, but spent summers on the Vineyard. Always it was a disappointment to me if the summer passed by and I had not seen and exchanged at least a word of greeting with my old Sunday School teacher. I missed it all the year.

Now I must tell about the last time I saw him. He was in poor health, and they said his mind had failed. I went to his house, and Mrs. Swift met me at the door. "Oh, Ruthie, I'm glad you've come. Will was speaking of you just the other day." She went on to tell me that while he did not seem to suffer, he did get confused, and she had to watch him all the time. Once she found him down where his store used to be, just sitting on the steps. He said he was waiting for customers, and then laughed all the way home. Several times she found him down at the church, always sitting in the last pew in the southwest corner. He was saying over and over to himself, "I just can't find the answer."

"Anyway, dear," she said to me, "come on in, and we'll hope he recognizes you. He just lies on the couch most of the time." She led me into the living room, and there he was on the couch. He had his eyes closed, and he looked thinner and grayer than when I had last seen him.

"Will," Mrs. Swift said to him cheerily, "Here's Ruth. You remember Ruth, don't you?"

"Oh, yes," he said, sitting up. "I remember Ruth. Here, sit down beside me. I'll make room."

"Now, that's nice," Mrs. Swift said. "You two have a nice chat while I see to my dinner."

I couldn't say a thing for the lump in my throat. I just put my face against his cheek and let the tears begin to flow.

"You mustn't cry," he said. "I'm very happy. I have much to think about, the long past, the long future."

"I don't know why I'm crying," I said. "I'm so happy to see you. Riv and the children send you their love — my love, you know, you've always had. You know that, don't you?"

"Oh, yes'" he said. "I know you love me. You always have."

Mrs. Swift called from the kitchen. "Ruthie, I want you to have a jar of my beets. It's the last of Will's garden, and they're so good with hash and beans. They're my own recipe, salt, sugar, cloves, and of course vinegar."

Later, as I was saying good-bye, Mr. Swift roused himself and said, "What was the last thing Jo said she put in the beets?"

"Vinegar, I said.

"Not *w*inegar!"

"No, not *w*inegar," I said, and we both laughed.

Then, as Mrs. Swift was seeing me to the door, Mr. Swift called out, "Jo, ask Ruthie how's her rheumatism."

"Why, my dear," she said, suddenly concerned, "I didn't know you had rheumatism!"

"No, I don't," I said suddenly remembering. "Not any more."

And so it was, a laugh and a joke that belonged to just us two. I have the memory of his laughter outweighing my moments of grieving, and with my heart I sing with the poet, "O Laughter, there are dimples enough in thy cheeks to catch and hold and glorify all the tears of grief. . . ."

AFTERWORD

by Eliot Eldridge Macy

In 1906 George "sold" the *Tidebook* to Mary and Gratia for one dollar, and the two girls, Mary principally, managed its publication for the next nine years. Then Ruth's husband, Wilfrid White, became publisher.

George died in 1914 at seventy, Sydna in 1936 at almost ninety. The four sisters left the Vineyard and went their separate ways.

Nina taught school in Wyoming, ran a church camp in Alabama, studied music, then taught it in a mountain school in Tennessee, became a laboratory technician, and, finally, when trouble with her eyes made her give up microscope work, became a social worker. While in Wyoming she learned to ride the range, on a visit home quite shocked the Vineyarders by mounting astride rather than sitting the customary sidesaddle. Nina had many admirers, and her love affairs were passionate and tempestuous, but she

never married. Always the scholar, she astounded her
nephews and nieces by reading the entire Bible in Spanish
— just because she wanted to.

When she retired in 1944 at the age of 66, she came home
to the Vineyard. Home was now Fourway. It was formerly
the old Owen stable and had since been converted into four
apartments. The sisters had bought it just the year before
with money inherited from Sydna, an apartment for each.
Who could tell, they might all return to the Vineyard to live
one day. In any event, here Nina spent her remaining
sixteen years rather quietly, passing the days with her
music, her books, her garden. She saw her sisters and their
families when they came to the Vineyard, but others she
saw only incidentally when she went to market or the post
office or the library. She was slender, straight-backed, to
many an awesome figure.

Mary had the major burden of the *Tidebook* for a while and
was unable to pursue her main interest, religion. But she
was determined. The summers of 1907 and 1908 she attended the Gordon Bible and Missionary Training School
in Boston. The following two summers she served as the
minister of a small Baptist Church in New Hope, Maine.
She did well enough, but in her mind she needed more
preparation. Next January she entered Hartford Theologi-
cal Seminary. There she met and, much to the dismay of the
seminary, became engaged to Paul Macy, a fellow student.
The seminary was afraid it might get the reputation for
running a martrimonial bureau and that this would affect
adversely its future endowments. Mary was told she would
have to leave the seminary. She was dreadfully disappointed, but consoled herself with the fact that her

husband-to-be would be a minister. Paul's first parish was the First Congregational Church in Ipswich, Massachusetts. The parsonage was a huge three-story house. Paul had his study on the top floor, but, the story goes, he was so in love with Mary he could hardly bear to stay up there and work on his sermons. After three years in Ipswich, Paul served parishes in Roxbury, Chicago, Toledo, Ohio, and Worcester, Massachusetts. A daughter was born in Ipswich, a son in Roxbury. Mary always took an active part in the church work. When Paul and she were in Toledo, the *Toledo Blade* wrote a feature article on her in a series of articles on the city's ten most prominent women. In Worcester she organized an association of Negro and white churchwomen that became citywide. After Paul died in 1960, Mary came home to the Vineyard. She was then eighty, but it never occurred to her that her work was done. Finding the Vineyard had no peace organization, she took it upon herself to form one. Paul and she had always been pacifists, and world peace was one of her deepest concerns. She died in January, 1978, at the age of ninety-seven just as the manuscript of this book was nearing completion. To the end she was still active in her peace work, busy writing letters, and getting others to, to oppose the B-1 bomber.

Ruth was sixteen when her father brought home with him from Boston a new handsome young assistant, recently from his native Australia. As Wilfrid Osborne White came up the walk, Ruth and her sisters were watching from the living room window. The others went to the door to meet him, but Ruth stole upstairs and "got herself all prettied up." Then she descended and made her entrance. Ruth and Riv were married five years later in 1904.

GRATIA: At the time of Ruth's wedding we lived down where Havenside now is, in a large Victorian house with a square tower. It was built by one of the whaling captains. It had double parlors. Cranberry was festooned all around the edge, mountain cranberry. Nina was maid of honor, and Mary and I were bridesmaids. Nina was dressed in a light blue silk muslin, Mary was in pink, and I had a sort of yellow-gold silk muslin. Ruth, of course, was in white. We came down the staircase and came across to the bay window where the ceremony took place. We thought Ruth was the whole show, so, contrary to custom, we allowed her to go first while we trailed after. . . .

For a while Riv worked as a compass adjuster for the Hutchinson Company in Boston, but then he went into business for himself, and in 1919 founded the Kelvin & Wilfrid O. White Company, which manufactured and re-tailed compasses and other nautical instruments. Ruth, meanwhile, was busy raising a family of two girls and two boys. But as soon as the youngest was in school, she had to look around for more to do. She was a lively person, her head teemed with ideas, and, true daughter of her mother, she didn't feel right unless she was busy. With the children in school, education was a natural focus for Ruth's attention. She had some creative ideas on the subject, and she saw a way to put them into practice. Riv and she had recently bought property at the Vineyard by Lake Tashmoo. It was the ideal place for a summer camp for youngsters, she thought. Hers, though, would be different from most camps, with their emphasis on competitive sports. At hers the emphasis would be on drama, music, and crafts.

For nine years during the twenties Ruth organized and ran Camp Tashmoo.

With the onset of the depression, Ruth became deeply concerned about the Vineyard economy. Having grown up here, she knew how hard it was for a young person to make a living even in the best of times. She tried various ways to encourage Island industry. She founded a garden center, then an arts and crafts center. (Auntie Ruth's projects! I remember thinking she dreamed them up just to keep my summer days busy lugging things, running errands, and, worst of all, weeding! But she made amends many times over. She was always doing me favors.)

In 1950 Ruth and Riv retired here. Not that that meant for Ruth slowing down. On the contrary, now she could give the Vineyard her year-round attention. How to improve the Island economy continued to be her principal concern. What was needed, she thought, was some new industry that would use some of the Vineyard's untapped resources. She had charmed many a palate with her beach plum jams and jellies. What about the beach plum? Using her considerable powers of persuasion, she got the state legislature to appropriate $500 a year for beach plum research. When research bogged down in the state laboratories, she lured the horticulturist-in-charge down to the Vineyard to work full time on beach plum propagation. It was a worthwhile try, but in the end the beach plum was found not to be feasible as a commercial crop. Then, still several years before it became a popular thing, she hit on pottery. This had a twofold appeal to her, as a naturalist and as an artist. The clay would come from the Vineyard's own soil, and the pottery would be decorated with old Vineyard designs. She took courses at the Museum School in Boston and established her own pottery studio. She brought professionals to the Vineyard to teach others. She remained active with her pottery until shortly before her death in 1967. Riv had died in 1955.

And Gratia? It was George's idea that Gratia could complete her education by staying home and reading the dictionary. Gratia, however, wanted to go to Wheaton College. Of the four girls she was the least in awe of her father, and made life intolerable around the house until he finally consented to let her go.

"I arrived at school clad in an Oxford gray raincoat that came down to my toes, a marvelous velvet hat with bird wings on it, and a motoring veil that Mother, in a rare burst of extravagance — she was by nature very thrifty — had bought for me. Of course I didn't motor, but everyone had a motoring veil whether she motored or not. It went around the hat, then tied in back, and then you tied a bow under your chin."

She finished the two-year course in 1906, and the following fall went to work on the *Tidebook* with Mary.

An important part of the *Tidebook* work was getting the advertisements. The sisters traveled from Maine to Philadelphia soliciting from chandleries, boatyards, sailmakers, and other marine suppliers. And they hated it.

"We were awful scared. But Mary would go in, and I would slink in after her, practically hanging on her skirts. If we lost an ad, we'd be terribly down, and we'd go and have an ice cream soda to cheer us up. If we got the ad, then we'd have a soda to celebrate. . . "

But Gratia wanted to further her education. She left the *Tidebook* to Mary, and in February, 1909, entered Teachers'

College at Columbia. She took her degree in physical education. In March, 1912, Bloomingdale Hospital in White
Plains, New York, hired her as its physical director. Milton
Harrington was a young psychiatrist on the staff. The moment Gratia saw him, she had a prophetic thought: Here is
the man I am going to marry. At first they were just good
friends. It wasn't until Milton went away to World War I
and came back that things became serious between them.
In 1920 they were married. The wedding was held at Ruth
and Riv's spacious Greek revival house in Waban, Massachusetts. Mary's Paul officiated.

"I came down the stairs with Mother, who was to give me
away. She looked lovely in a gray silk gown. I wore a white
satin gown with what they call a chapel train, a square train
that fell from the waist. After the ceremony we danced a
Virginia Reel, which is an old wedding dance. My friends
said they'd never forget the sight of me dancing the Virginia Reel with my wedding dress train over my arm! My
going-away costume was a brownish olive — I have it still,
everything, suit, blouse, even the spats. We wore spats at
that time. The spats and the skirt met about seven inches off
the ground. I wore with it a black velvet hat, a three-
cornered one with a topknot of blue-and-pink ribbon."

Milton divided his time between private practice as a
psychiatrist and writing. In 1938 he published his major
work, *A Biological Approach to the Problem of Abnormal Be-
havior*. Shortly afterwards he suffered a coronary attack,
from which he never fully recovered. He died in 1942.

Gratia had to go to work. Her one child, an adopted
daughter, was already grown. It was World War II, and
jobs were plentiful even for women in their late fifties. Her
first job was in Boston working for an organization set up to

provide hospitality for British officers and servicemen when their ships were in port. When that job ended with the end of the war, she got the job as director of activities for Peabody House, a Boston settlement house. In 1949 she moved to New York and became director of volunteers at Metropolitan Hospital. She held this post nine years, and in 1956, at the age of seventy-one, retired to the Vineyard.

While in most things Ruth and Gratia were miles apart, they especially shared the Eldridge antipathy to inaction. Upon Gratia's arrival at the Vineyard she immediately got busy in Fourway's extensive garden. If a man was not handy to do spade work, she did it herself. She had always been an avid reader, and she joined the Want-to-Know Club and Great Books. She also joined SANE and the League of Women Voters. Civic duty is one thing she took, and takes, most seriously. Every time an attempt is made to make Vineyard Haven wet, Gratia organizes the opposition and puts the wets to rout. (Many who imbibe nevertheless prefer to keep Vineyard Haven the way it is, dry.) When Gratia speaks in town meeting, people listen. Eighty some years ago Benny Crowell — on whose hammock she delighted to do her acrobatics — nicknamed Gratia "Grittiny." It was soon shortened to just plain "Gritty." Last year Gratia suddenly disappeared from the Vineyard, telling only Mary and a niece where she was going. Two weeks later she returned from a twelve-day tour of Hong Kong!

Looking back I try to think of the way it must have been. I can't help wondering about George, my grandfather. Maybe it was a good thing he had to be in Boston much of the time. Such a phalanx of powerful women, and he the only man. . . .

Appendix I
ELDRIDGE TIDE & PILOT BOOK

As recounted in the Foreword, the *Eldridge Tide and Pilot Book* had its origin in an accident aboard his schooner during a storm that disabled George Eldridge and prevented his ever going to sea again. It also gave him such a horror of marine disasters and their effect on human lives that he determined to help others avert them. Several months after his accident at sea, another severe storm created dangerous shoal conditions off Chatham, and George set out, as soon as he was able, to make a large-scale chart of this new marine hazard as a guide and warning to mariners sailing that way. The event is described in his first issue of what was then called the *Eldridge Coastal Pilot:*

In April, 1851, an inlet was opened by the furious storm waves through Nauset Beach, about 1½ miles northeasterly from Chatham Lighthouse. The current of Ebb, by its strength and velocity, has carried seaward into deep water a large quantity of sand, forming dangerous shoals called Chatham New Harbor Bars, which lie in the direct track of vessels (especially with off-shore winds) bound east or west by way of Vineyard Sound. A nun Buoy has been placed off these Bars, but at night-time, with a smooth sea, there are neither marks nor bearings to warn the mariner of his approach to these dangerous shoals and he is liable to mistake the mainland for the beach, the latter being very deceptive on account of its being elevated, but very little from the shore. The above facts, together with my personal experience and observations, show these bars to be the most dangerous spot on the coast of the United States.

He showed the finished chart to seafaring friends, who immediately realized the value of it. It was published that same year, launching what was to grow into a compendium of practical information that became indispensable to yachtsmen, pilots, and fishermen. "I wouldn't go to sea without Eldridge" is a phrase common among them.

For forty-seven years his charts were financed and sold by S. Thaxter & Sons. In all, he published fourteen different charts, each of which was continually revised. He also made use of existing charts, published by the Federal Government since 1844, enlarging them for visual clarity and supplementing them with vital navigational information of his own finding. In 1880 a display of Eldridge publications, charts, and pilot books was awarded first prize at the International Fishery Exhibition in Germany, and the next year the exhibit won first prize at the Massachusetts Mechanics Fair.

S. Thaxter & Sons also financed two editions of the *Eldridge Coastal Pilot*. These contained descriptions of ports, shoals, current notes, suggested courses, and other relevant information, compiled from all existing reference works of the time, and embellished with George Eldridge's personal observations of the New England coastline. The first of these was issued in 1853, and was to be the forerunner of the *Eldridge Tide & Pilot Book,* which began publication in 1875.

"Chart George" Eldridge was the first publisher of the *Tidebook*. In 1892, preoccupied with Chatham town affairs, he turned the publishing over to George W., his son. Mary and Gratia Eldridge were the publishers between 1906 and 1915. For the next forty years Ruth's husband, Wilfrid O. White, was publisher. Today the publisher is Robert Eldridge White, great-grandson of "Chart George."

Appendix II

Vineyard Haven Herald, Thursday, December 1, 1898

GREATEST STORM OF THE XIX CENTURY

A TERRIBLE DISASTER VISITS THE ISLAND

Last Saturday night and Sunday recorded a storm which for its fearful and terrible effect will be memorable on this Island as the greatest storm of the nineteenth century. The older inhabitants were in the habit of quoting the storm of 1878 as the most fearful that had ever visited the Island, a northeaster like the one just past, driving 23 vessels on the shores of the harbor and by a curious coincidence a schooner was driven through Norris's wharf, Eastville, in a similar manner to the picturesque destruction at Union Wharf, but the storm, severe and damaging as it proved, was mild in comparison to the November storm of 1898 — 38 vessels either sunk, ashore, or more or less damaged, with eight lives lost, and but for the rescue of twenty or more sailors by the extraordinary bravery of our citizens, the death toll would have been appalling.

About dusk on Saturday evening the wind, which had been moderate from the northeast all day, increased rapidly in force and with it a sprinkling of snow commenced which soon turned into rain. Storm signals all along the coast had warned vessels into harbor, and all day long coasting schooners dropped anchor in Vineyard Harbor. With the night the wind rose higher and higher until it reached the velocity of 54 miles; the snow had turned to rain, which fell in torrents during the night, changing into snow about daylight. Sometime during the night some vessel yet unknown broke her anchorage and drifted into vessel after vessel, breaking other anchor lines and creating a fearful confusion amidst the fury of the storm. The snow was so thick that but little of the harbor could be seen from the land until with a violent suddenness about half-past ten on Sunday morning the storm lifted and the sun shone out with marvelous beauty, revealing a wreck-strewn harbor. Wherever one looked a dismasted or sunken or stranded vessel could be seen. The east side of the harbor was liter- ally lined with vessels, and each shoal spot along the chan- nel was marked by some unfortunate victim of the disaster. At the Union Wharf the large three-masted schooner *Newburg* was driven by the force of the wind and waves across the flats and into and through the wharf 15 feet from shore, carrying a hundred feet of that structure. Hundreds visited the scene of the wreckage along the beach on Mon- day morning, and from Norris's wharf to Chadwick's blacksmith shop a scene was presented of a vast lum- beryard struck by a cyclone; every foot of the way was covered with lumber and laths which had been the deck loads of several schooners, and it is estimated that equiva- lent to one million feet of lumber was strewn along the beach, and mingled with it here and there were articles of ship furniture, mattresses, provisions of all sorts, which came from the schooners which broke up under the force of the waves. The telephone and electric poles were flat down on the road, with the wires in inextricable confusion, and all day long men and teams were at work gathering and piling up the salvage. It was a sad and terrible sight of destruction, and evidenced the force of the storm, but the remarkable fact is noticed that the roadbed, usually undermined and torn up by the waves, is entirely unharmed save by the stones and debris thrown over the concrete.

It would take a volume to record the heroic deeds that occurred, but some are worthy of being emblazoned in letters of gold. During Sunday afternoon word came to the village of Vineyard Haven that several crews of sunken vessels were in the rigging exhausted and in momentary danger of being washed overboard and drowned. Dr. Tabb of the Marine Hospital, who worked as hard as any surgeon on the bloody field of El Caney, suggested the organization of a lifesaving rescue party. Several tugs were solicited to take the men and a dory. Two of the tugs were so anchored that they feared to make the attempt, but the gallant Capt. Wentworth of the tug *Lockhart,* anchored at the wharf, who, to escape being crushed by the *Newburg* bearing down on him, had moved forward only to be driven on the piles which carried away his port rail and twisted his stem, volunteered to take them. The plan was for the tug to get to windward of the wrecked vessels and drift the dory to them by line and haul them to the tug. But on arriving at the scene, the crowd of vessels to windward, with dense darkness and drifting snow, prevented this plan, and the tug could not reach nearer than a quarter of a mile. The crew, consisting of Isaac C. Norton, Postmaster F. Horton Johnson, and Alvin H. Cleveland, who have a proud record as wreckers in former storms, without thought of the risk of attempting the rescue in an open dory, jumped in and cast loose from the tug. They reached the schooner *Annie A. Booth,* where six men were rescued. The captain said he and his men were too exhausted to risk landing through the surf, and begged to be put on board the schooner *S.C. Hart*, which was near, Capt. Eaton hauling the men up one at a time in a bowline over the yawl at the stern. This the crew accomplished, and then attempted to reach the schooner *L. H. Thurlow*, but with all their strength they could make no progress toward her and were compelled to land through the surf on the beach and drag the dory to windward of the ill-fated vessels, whose captain, lashed to the mast, was already dead from exposure, being an old man in delicate health. At the beach, Stanley Fisher of East Chop Light joined the crew and together they put off and rescued the remaining five of the crew and landed them safely through the surf, where Surgeon Tabb with his hospital corps was waiting to take them to the residence of Capt. S. H. Norton, where everything was done for their comfort. During Sunday morning, Isaac C. Norton, Alvin H. Cleveland, and Frank Golart put off in a dory from near Judge Arnoux's place, and with superhuman strength and against the judgment of all onlookers, reached the schooner *E. J. Hamilton* and rescued five men, landing them safely on the beach below the marine railway.

The schooner *Canaria*, during the storm Sunday morning, saw a small schooner sinking to leeward of them. The captain, with that courage which is now known as American, slipped his anchor and drifted with the storm alongside, and so skillfully was it done that the crew of five men easily jumped aboard his craft and were saved, as the *Canaria* drifted ashore near the Lagoon bridge. Another three-masted schooner, the *Lizzie Wallace*, performed a similar feat, and drifted alongside a sinking vessel, rescuing the crew of 13 men, and drifted ashore near the *Canaria*.

These are a few of the acts of heroism that make Americans proud of their race.

But we have to record a pathetic picture of failure to rescue under circumstances and conditions impossible to overcome. The *Island City* went ashore near the opening into Lake Anthony between Highland Wharf and Oak Bluffs Wharf. Promptly Capt. Bunker organized a crew and secured a dory. Frank Bunker, Fred James, Edward Silvey, Walter Carter, Trueman Galley, Benjamin Davis, Willie Givens, and Walter Pierce all made several attempts to launch the dory; a crowd of thirty men were there to help. The storm and waves at this point were more powerful than in the harbor, being exposed to the open sea. Every attempt to launch the dory failed, with serious danger to the men. The crowd would rush the dory into the surf up to their armpits, but each time the waves dashed the dory back on the beach as if it was a toy boat. The men on the schooner were exhausted and had evidently lost their heads. Signals were made to them to jump, but they paid no attention, seeming to act dazed. If they had jumped, a line of men was to be formed into the surf to catch them, but nothing could be done. Frank Marshall tried to throw a line with ordinary rockets, but it would not carry, and the crowd on the beach had to witness the perishing of the crew one by one. A sailor who had stuck to the boom for hours created a ripple of hope when he moved to the deck as if to get a line and jump. He was seen to drop onto the deck and a few minutes later his head appeared above the bulwarks, but he dropped and was seen no more until taken off drowned in the hold. It was a pitiful sight, and emphasizes the need of the Massachusetts Humane Society to furnish this Island with a lifeboat and a gun to fire a lifeline. Later in the day, when the fury of the gale lessened, Frank P. Bunker, Fred James, and Walter T. Pierce went out and took a man from the rigging, but he had been dead some hours; another sailor's body floated ashore, but the captain and the fourth sailor have not been found.

In the afternoon, Capt. Bunker's crew rescued five men from the schooner *C.H.Raymond* near Norris's wharf, and another party, B.W. Pease, John Randolph, Wm. Maury, and Morton Wills rescued five men from *Pefetto* at daylight Monday, who were taken to Capt. Daggett's, and citizens of Cottage City furnished clothing.

Cottage City suffered considerably in the matter of injury to buildings and cottages. Carpenter's barn is flat to the ground, with a valuable lot of carriages smashed under the building. The house and barn moved by Mr. Niles from Lagoon Heights to Nashawena Park lies a pile of lumber, roofs are stripped of shingles and skylights; wherever you walk you see signs down, windows and doors broken in, ornaments and piazza railings blown down, and about twenty chimneys toppled over. The chimney at the residence of Mr. G.B. Holbrook fell upon the roof, doing considerable damage. The *Herald* roof and chimney sustained considerable damage. The chimney of the Naumkeag fell upon the roof, smashing a big hole, and the chimney of the Oak Bluffs Club fell, demolishing the kitchen, while the chimney at Mr. Claypool's fell outside, the only damage done being to a few shingles and a meeting board. The railing and scroll work on Ginn's block lies in the avenue, and the tower on the east end of the building has been loosened from its foundations and is in danger of falling in the next high wind. The Nash cottage is stripped of its gingerbread work, and the fences are flat.   The Pierce villa is considerably damaged, one end being blown down. About half of Ellinwood's bridge is blown away, leaving the bare spiles. Fifty feet of the railroad bridge at Sengekontacket opening were carried away, but the carriage bridge escaped, except that a hole at the end of ten feet of earth was washed but quickly repaired so that travel was interrupted but one day. But marks of the storm are to be seen on every side, as few cottages escaped some slight damage. An old wreck near Norris's wharf, against which the owners were warned, was dashed by the waves through the wharf, doing serious damage.

Photographers, professional and amateur, are reaping a rich harvest of interesting sights that will be much in demand from summer residents next season.

Following this terrific gale another snowstorm of some magnitude broke over the Island on Wednesday, stopping the mail stages and travel, and preventing the steamers from making their trip, but no damage is reported.

Courtesy of the Vineyard Gazette